Every Day Gratitude Journal

This journal belongs to

____

Molly McLuke

TODAY I'M GRATEFUL FOR

I'm thankful for:

____

____

____

Goals and dreams I achieved:

____

____

____

What I'm looking forward to:

____

____

____

SELF-CARE Q&A

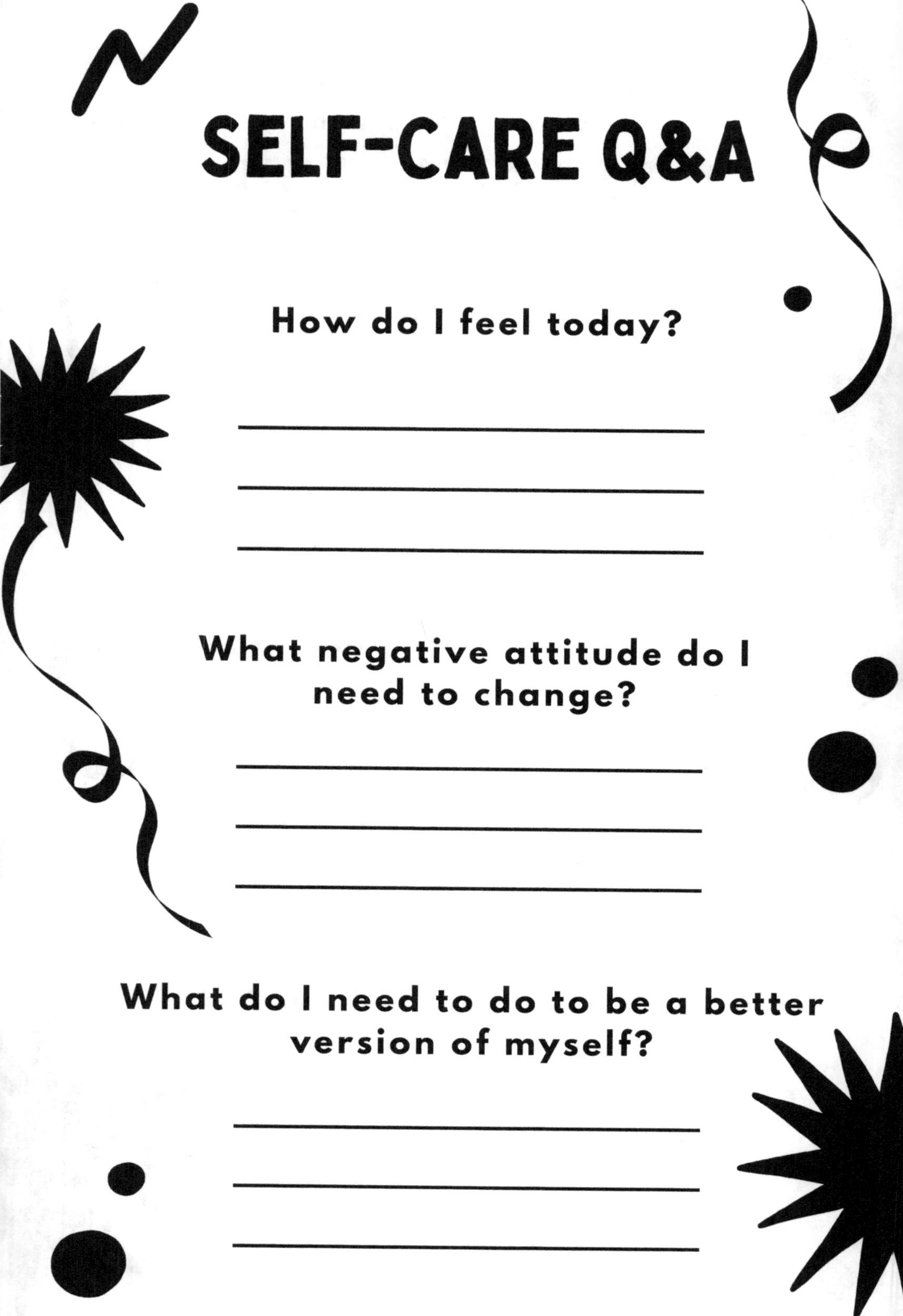

How do I feel today?

____

____

____

What negative attitude do I need to change?

____

____

____

What do I need to do to be a better version of myself?

____

____

TODAY I'M GRATEFUL FOR

I'm thankful for:

____

____

____

Goals and dreams I achieved:

____

____

____

What I'm looking forward to:

____

____

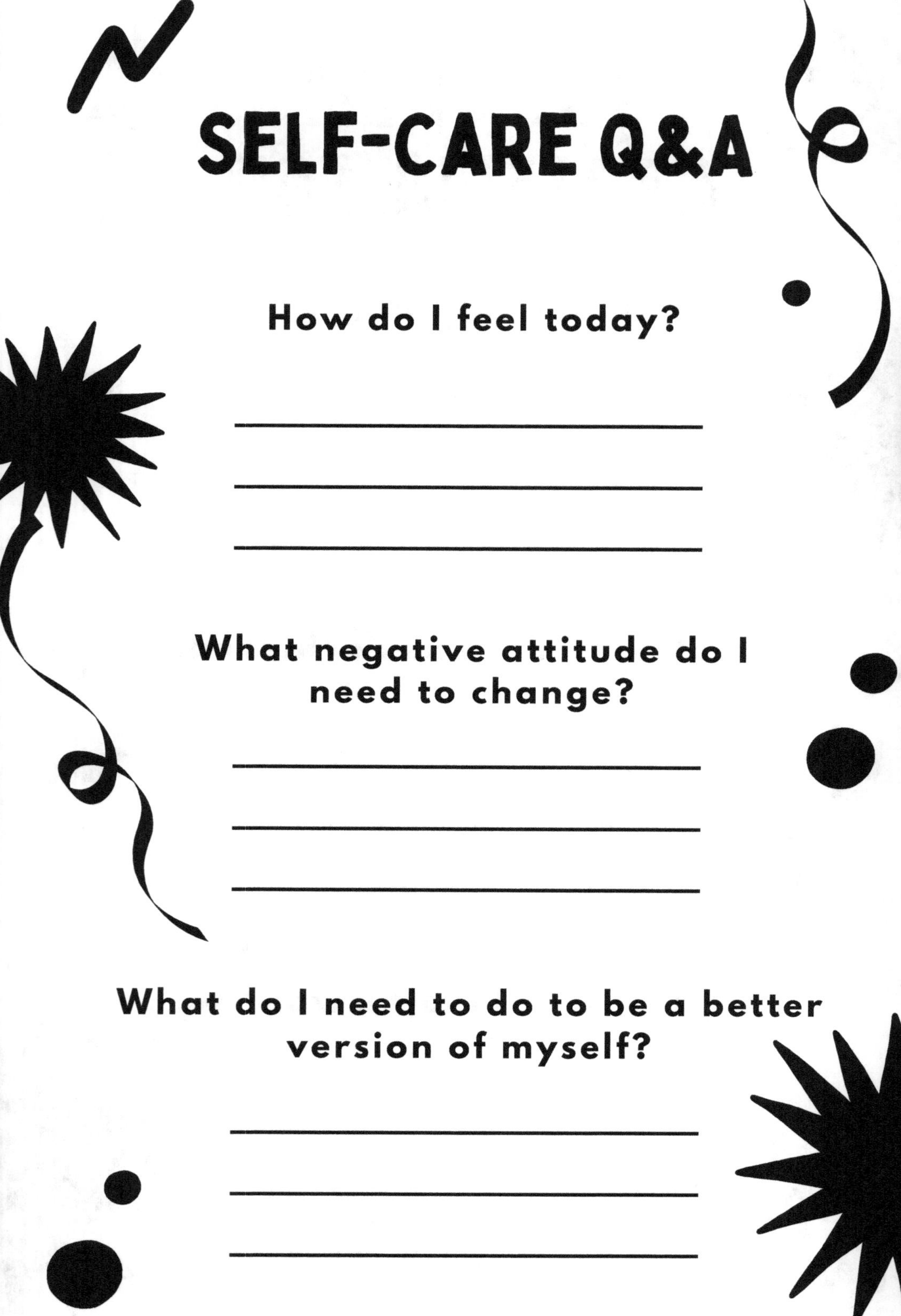

SELF-CARE Q&A

How do I feel today?

What negative attitude do I need to change?

What do I need to do to be a better version of myself?

TODAY I'M GRATEFUL FOR

I'm thankful for:

____

____

____

Goals and dreams I achieved:

____

____

____

What I'm looking forward to:

____

____

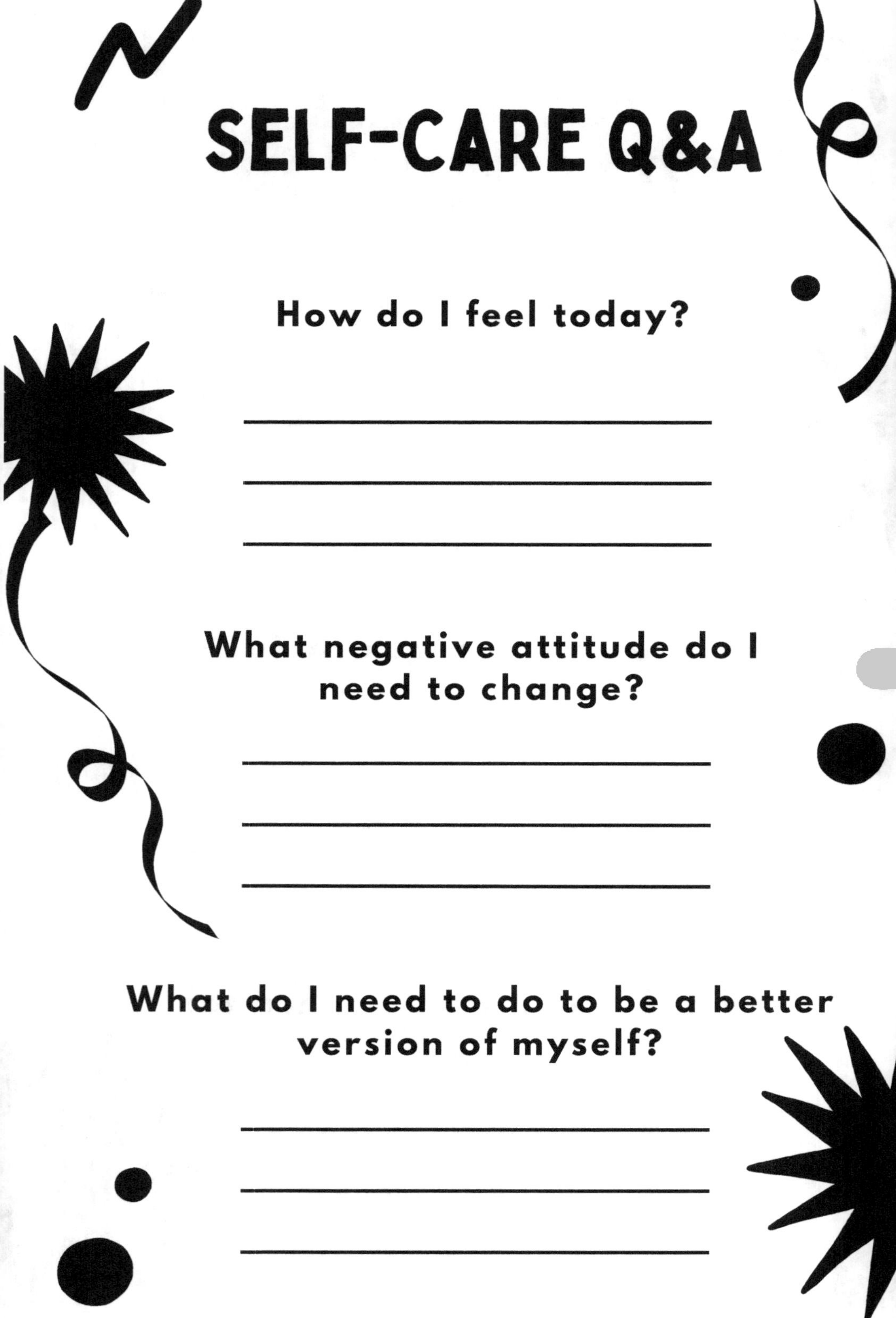

SELF-CARE Q&A

How do I feel today?

What negative attitude do I need to change?

What do I need to do to be a better version of myself?

TODAY I'M GRATEFUL FOR

I'm thankful for:

____

____

____

Goals and dreams I achieved:

____

____

____

What I'm looking forward to:

____

____

____

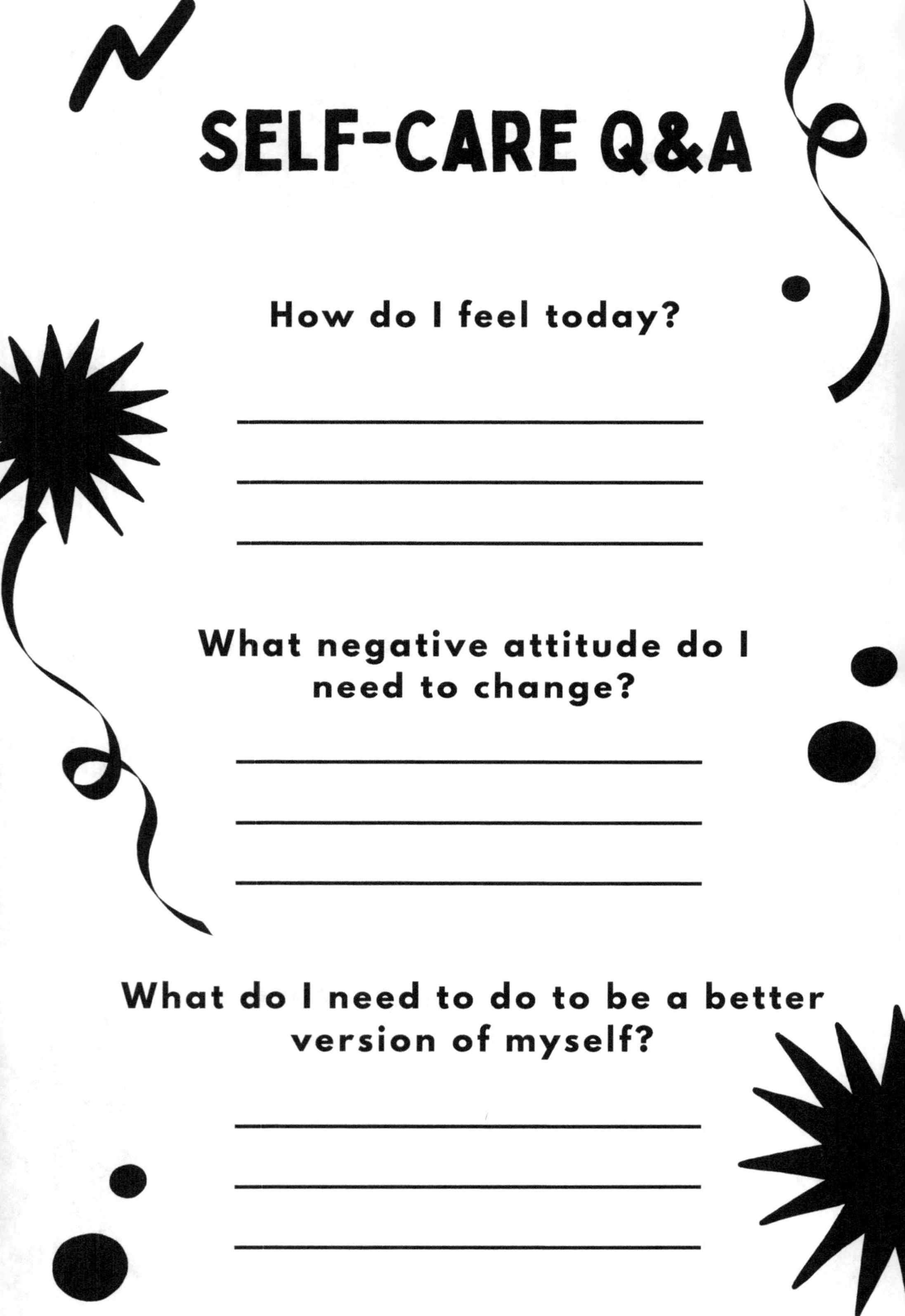

SELF-CARE Q&A

How do I feel today?

____

____

____

What negative attitude do I need to change?

____

____

____

What do I need to do to be a better version of myself?

____

____

____

TODAY I'M GRATEFUL FOR

I'm thankful for:

____

____

____

Goals and dreams I achieved:

____

____

____

What I'm looking forward to:

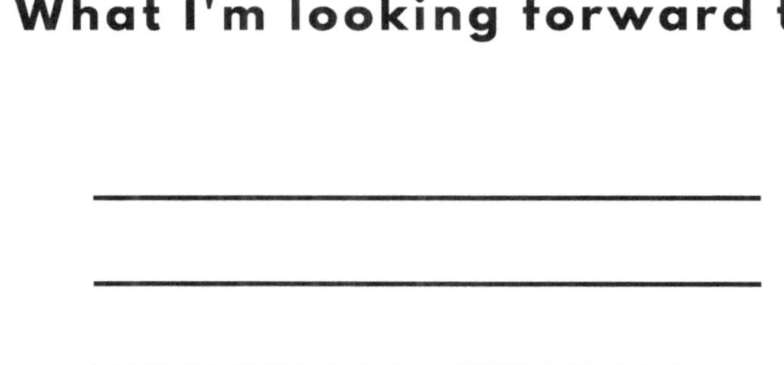

____

____

____

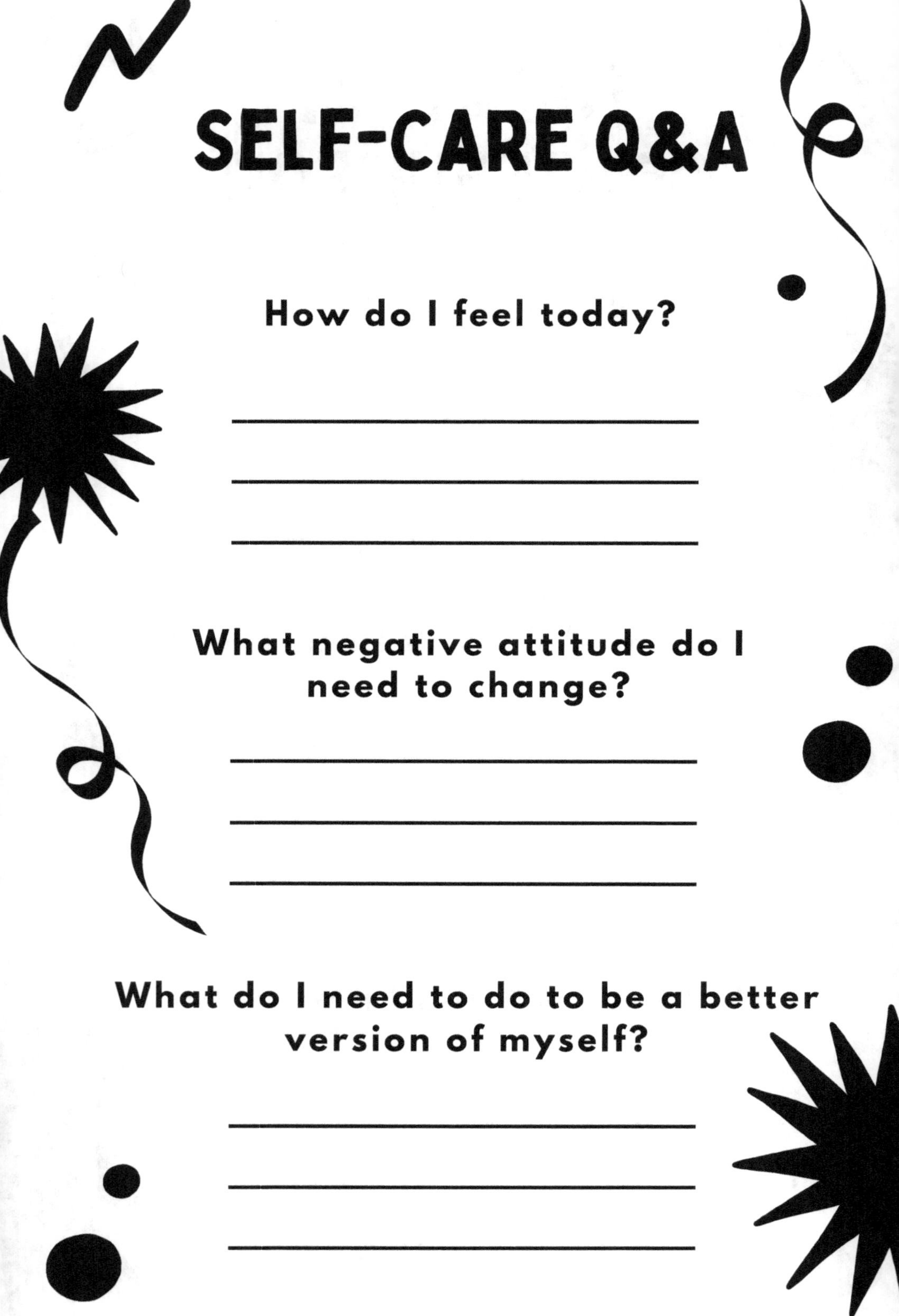

SELF-CARE Q&A

How do I feel today?

What negative attitude do I
need to change?

What do I need to do to be a better
version of myself?

TODAY I'M GRATEFUL FOR

I'm thankful for:

____

____

____

Goals and dreams I achieved:

____

____

____

What I'm looking forward to:

____

____

SELF-CARE Q&A

How do I feel today?

____

____

____

What negative attitude do I need to change?

____

____

____

What do I need to do to be a better version of myself?

____

____

TODAY I'M GRATEFUL FOR

I'm thankful for:

____

____

____

Goals and dreams I achieved:

____

____

____

What I'm looking forward to:

____

____

____

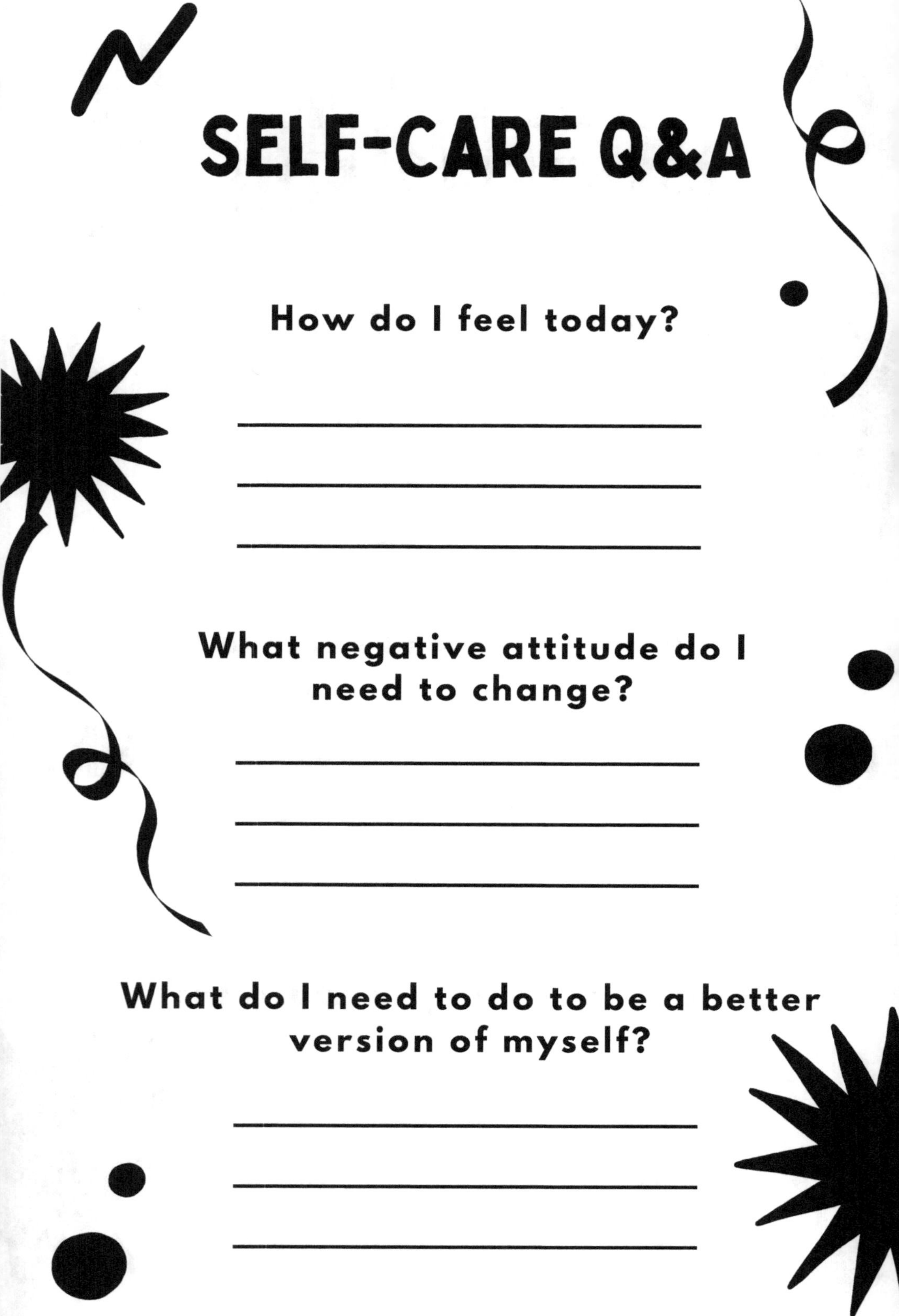

SELF-CARE Q&A

How do I feel today?

____

____

____

What negative attitude do I need to change?

____

____

____

What do I need to do to be a better version of myself?

____

____

____

TODAY I'M GRATEFUL FOR

I'm thankful for:

Goals and dreams I achieved:

What I'm looking forward to:

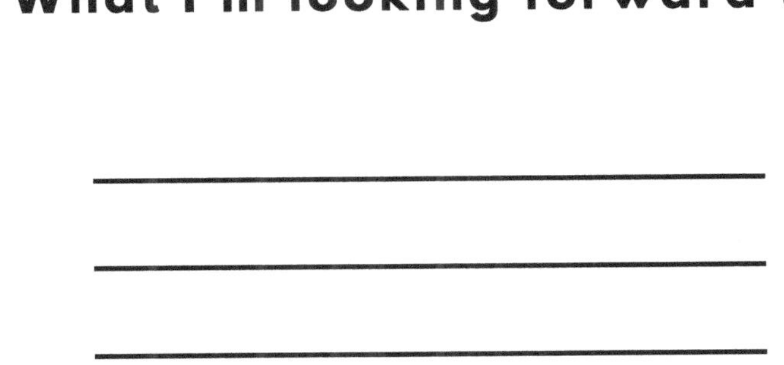

SELF-CARE Q&A

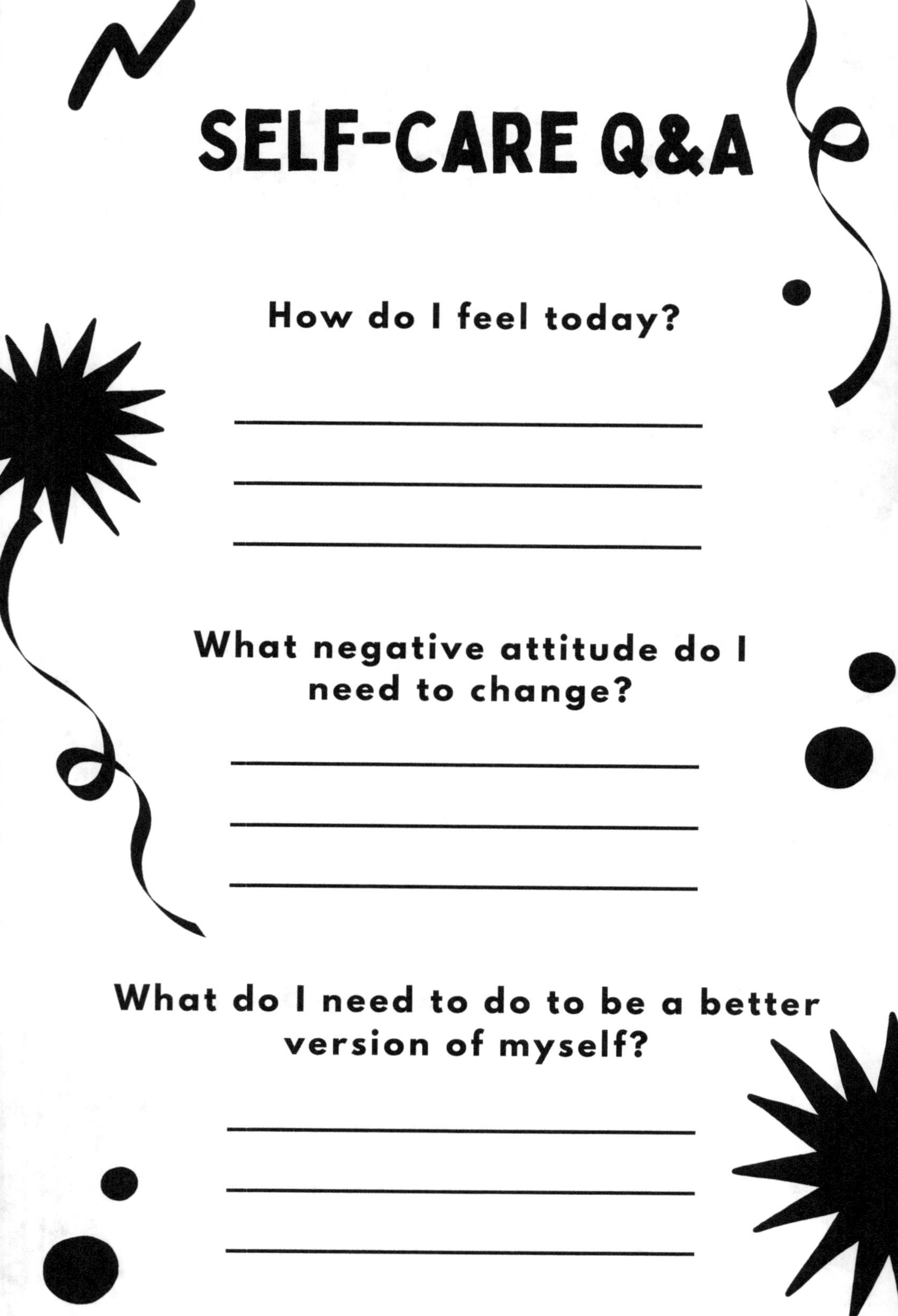

How do I feel today?

____

____

____

What negative attitude do I need to change?

____

____

____

What do I need to do to be a better version of myself?

____

____

TODAY I'M GRATEFUL FOR

I'm thankful for:

____

____

____

Goals and dreams I achieved:

____

____

____

What I'm looking forward to:

____

____

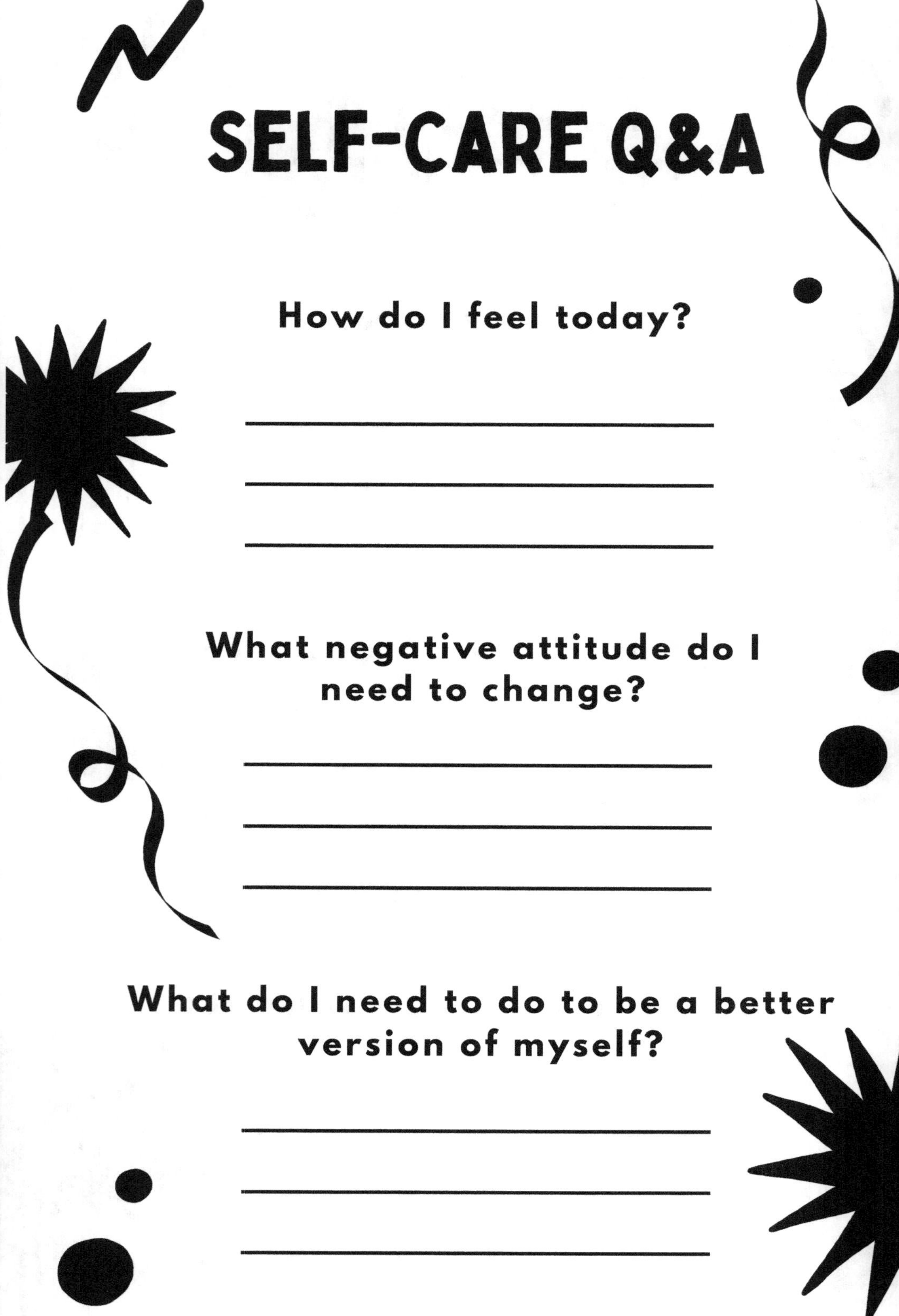

SELF-CARE Q&A

How do I feel today?

What negative attitude do I need to change?

What do I need to do to be a better version of myself?

TODAY I'M GRATEFUL FOR

I'm thankful for:

____

____

____

Goals and dreams I achieved:

____

____

____

What I'm looking forward to:

____

____

SELF-CARE Q&A

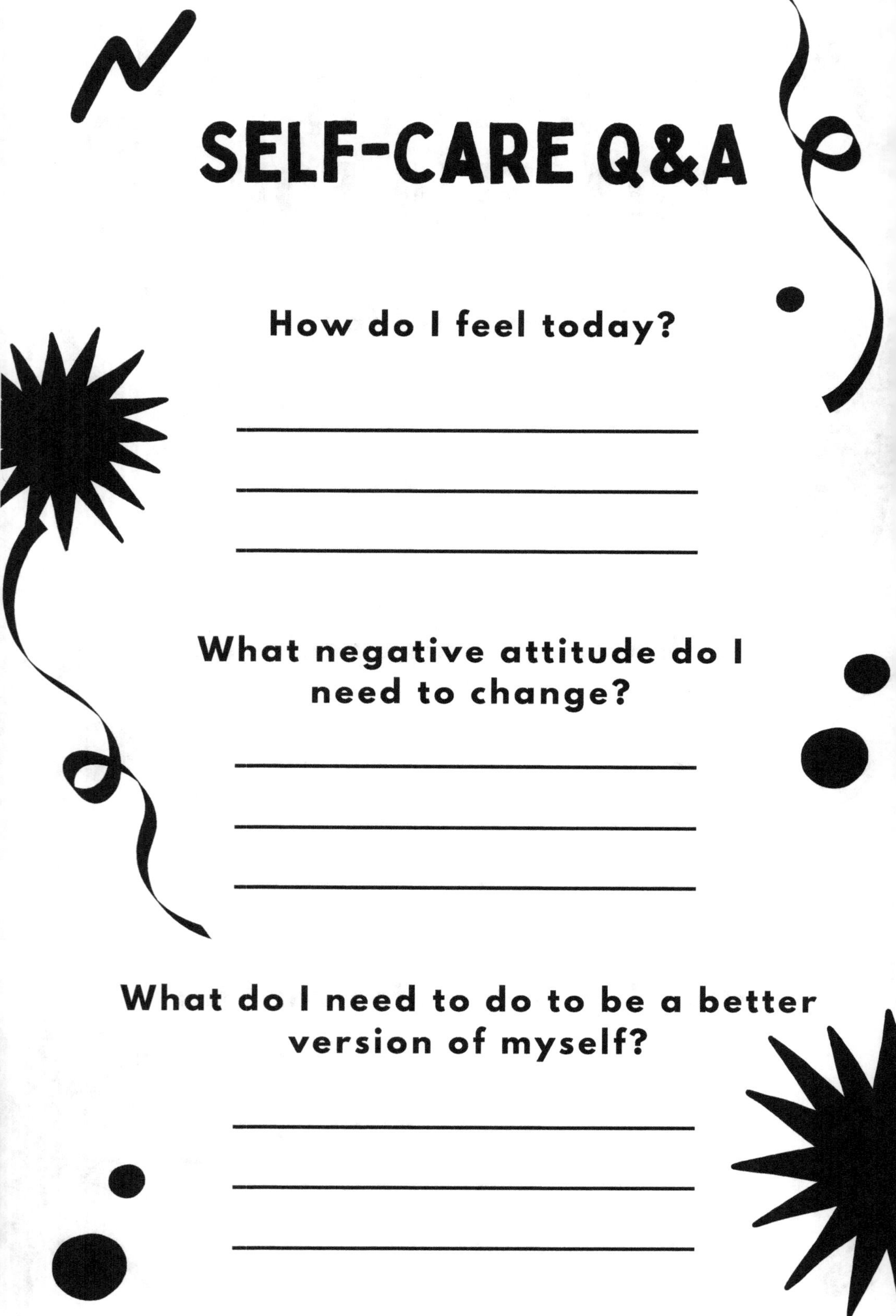

How do I feel today?

____

____

____

What negative attitude do I need to change?

____

____

____

What do I need to do to be a better version of myself?

____

____

____

TODAY I'M GRATEFUL FOR

I'm thankful for:

____

____

____

Goals and dreams I achieved:

What I'm looking forward to:

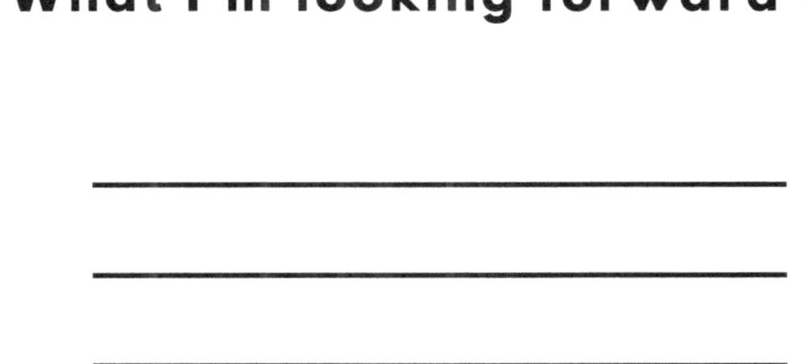

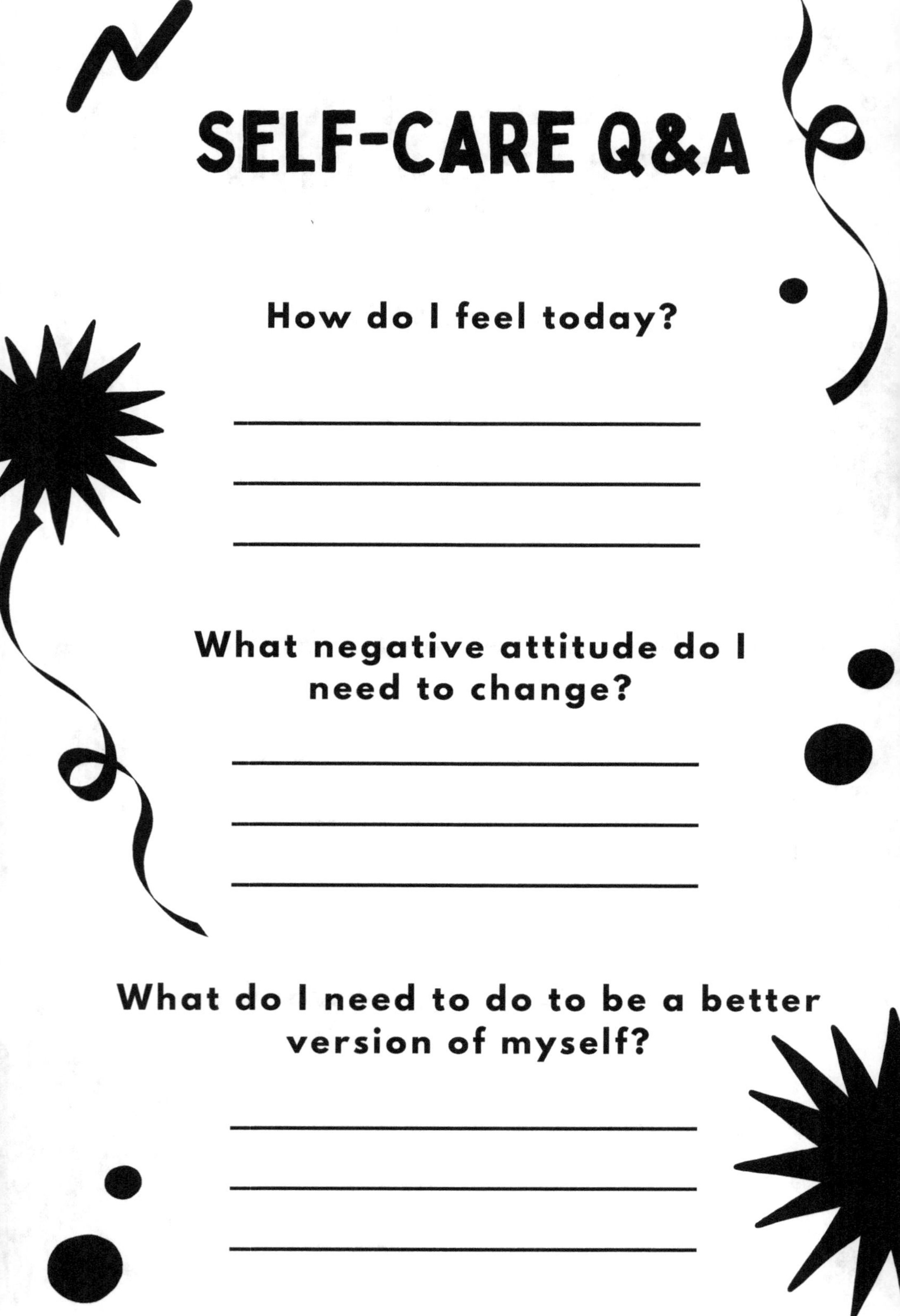

SELF-CARE Q&A

How do I feel today?

What negative attitude do I need to change?

What do I need to do to be a better version of myself?

TODAY I'M GRATEFUL FOR

I'm thankful for:

____

____

____

Goals and dreams I achieved:

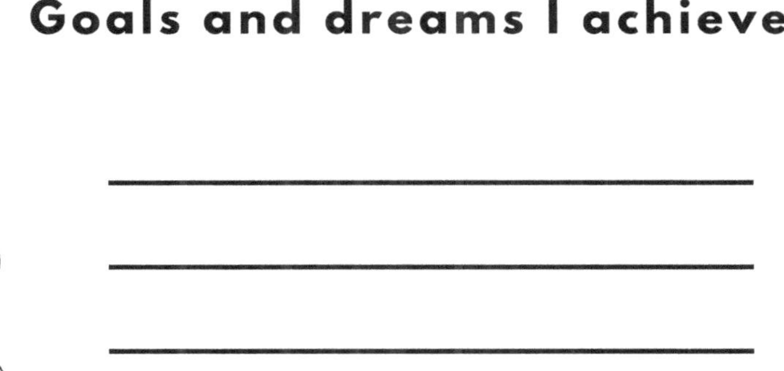

____

____

____

What I'm looking forward to:

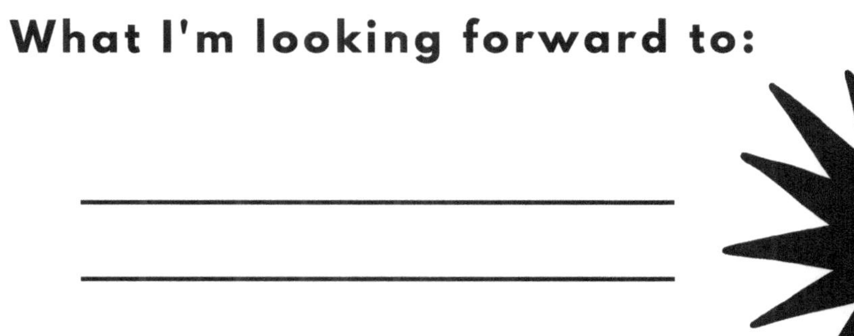

____

____

____

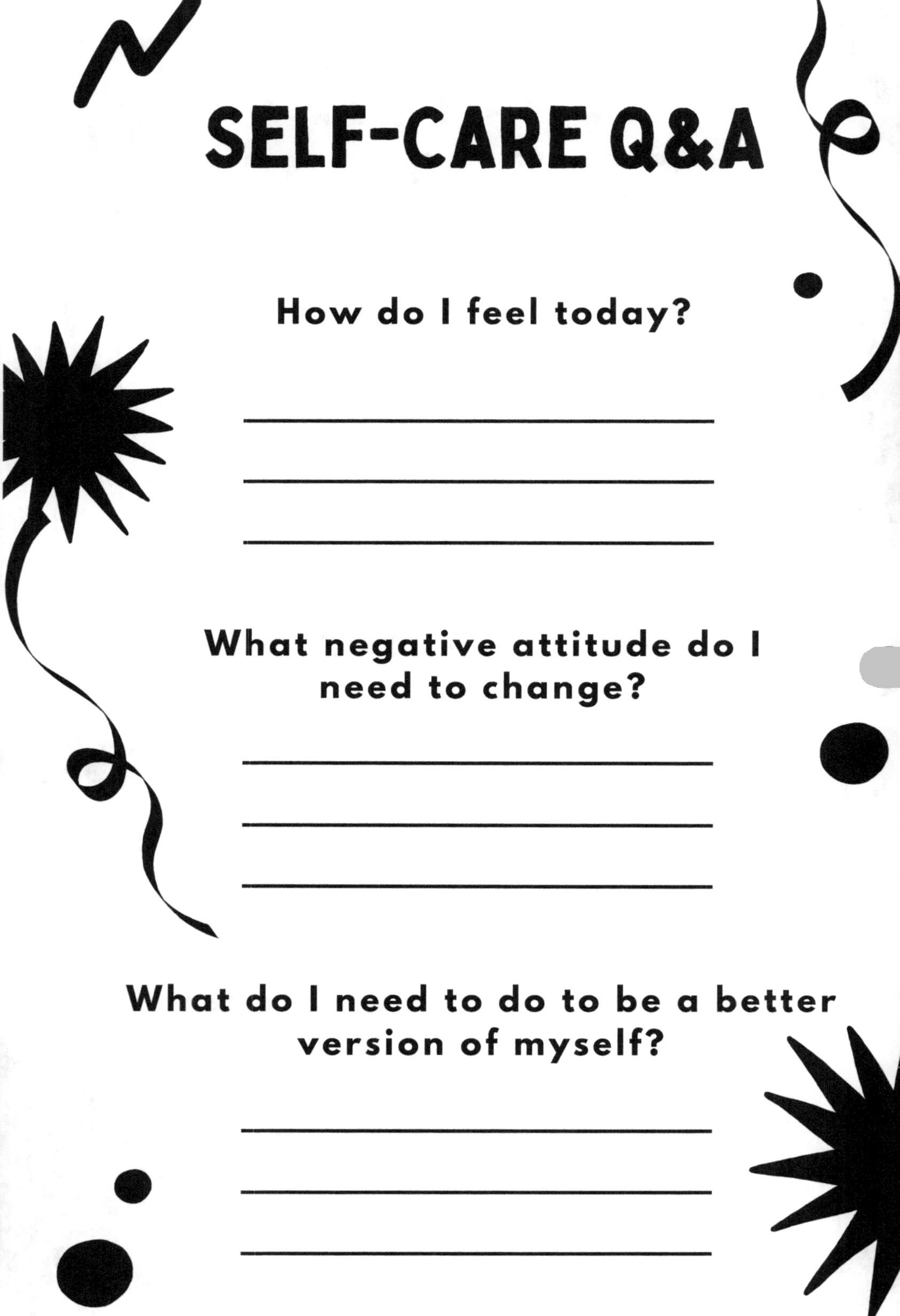

SELF-CARE Q&A

How do I feel today?

What negative attitude do I
need to change?

What do I need to do to be a better
version of myself?

TODAY I'M GRATEFUL FOR

I'm thankful for:

____

____

____

Goals and dreams I achieved:

____

____

____

What I'm looking forward to:

____

____

____

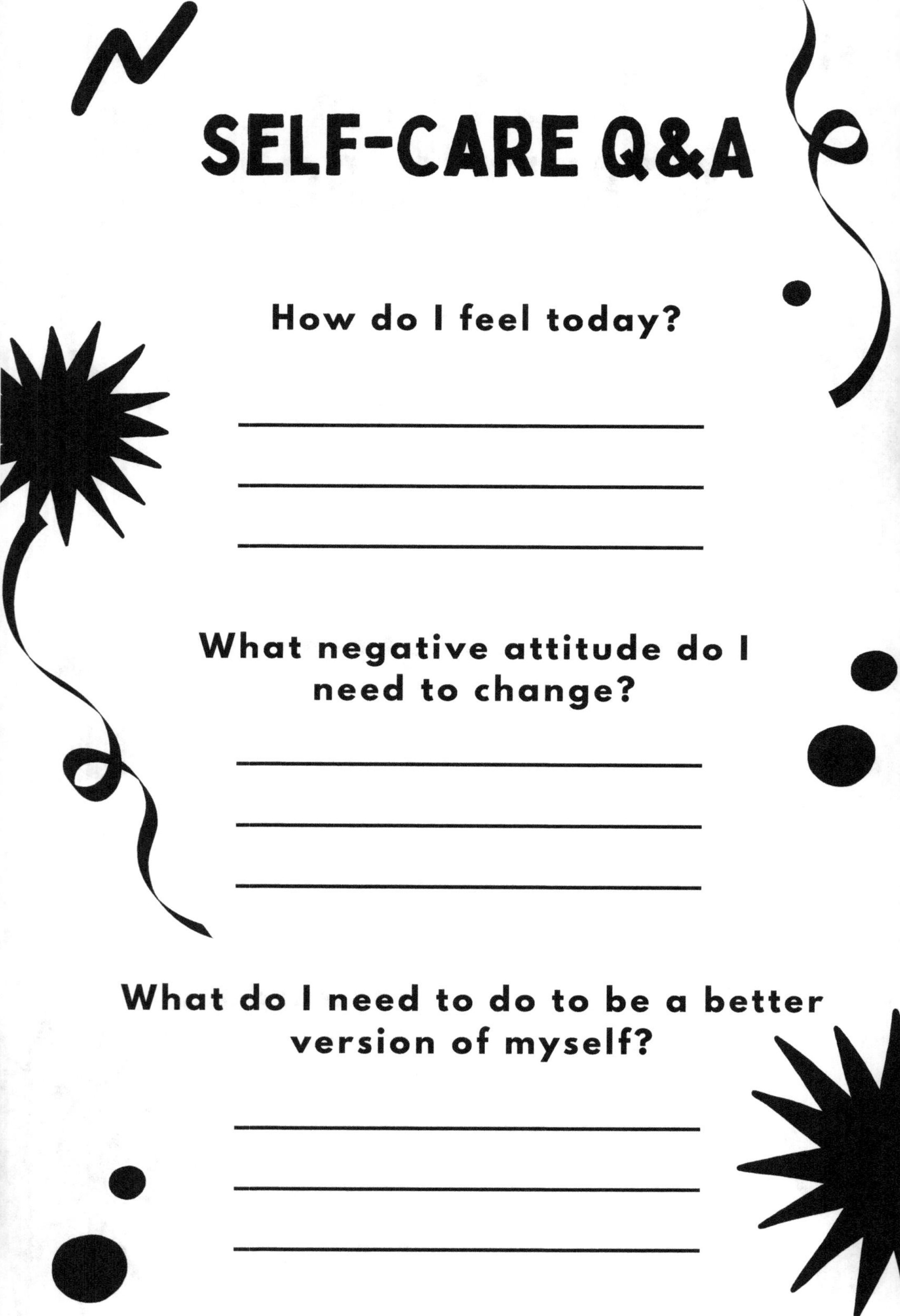

SELF-CARE Q&A

How do I feel today?

What negative attitude do I need to change?

What do I need to do to be a better version of myself?

TODAY I'M GRATEFUL FOR

I'm thankful for:

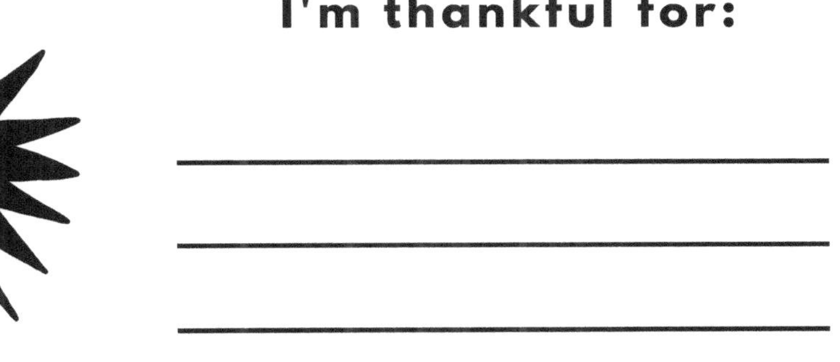

Goals and dreams I achieved:

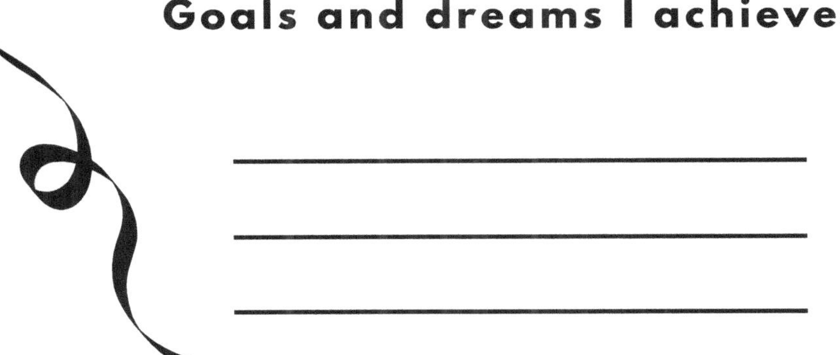

What I'm looking forward to:

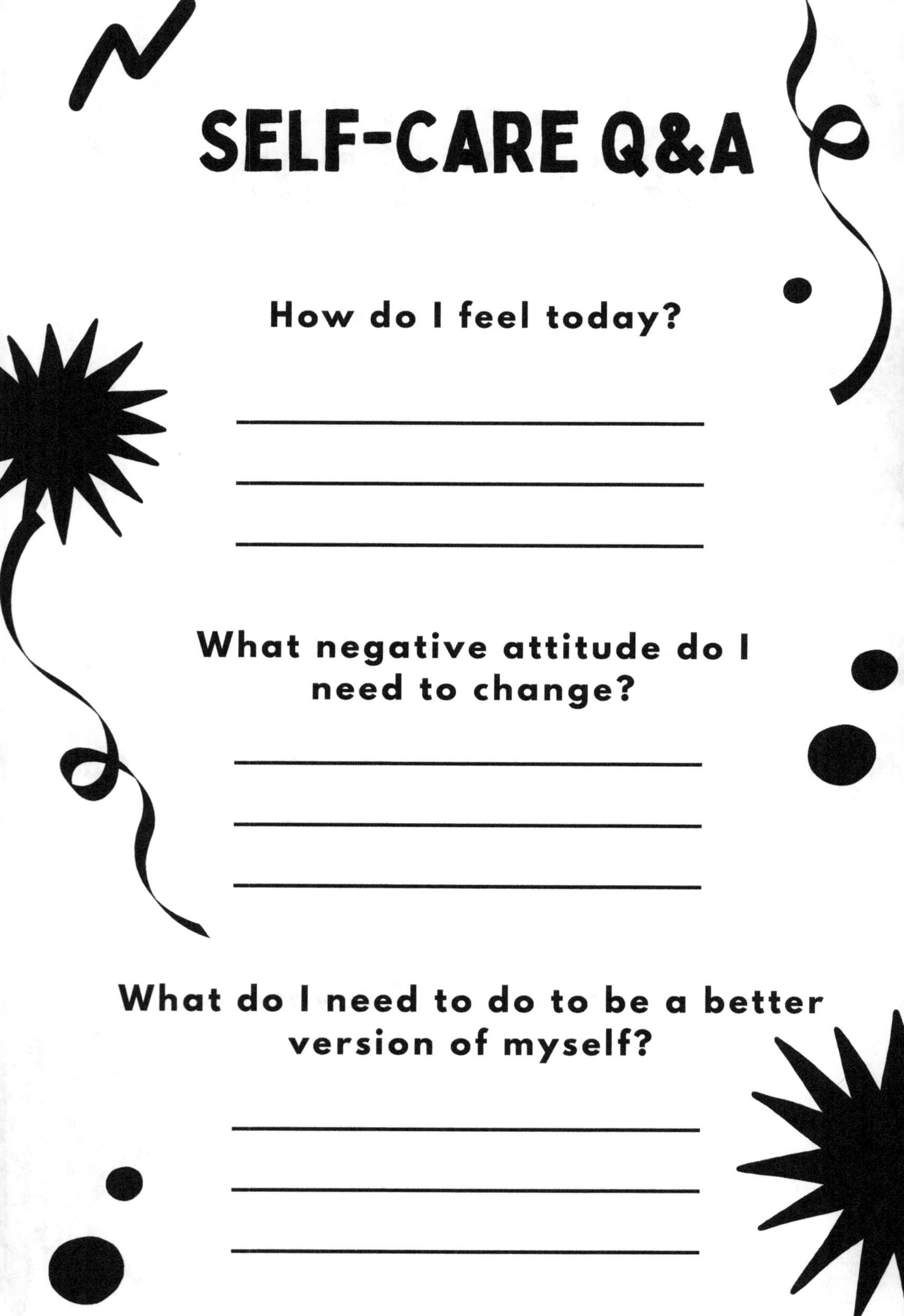

SELF-CARE Q&A
How do I feel today?
What negative attitude do I need to change?
What do I need to do to be a better version of myself?

TODAY I'M GRATEFUL FOR

I'm thankful for:

____

____

____

Goals and dreams I achieved:

____

____

____

What I'm looking forward to:

____

____

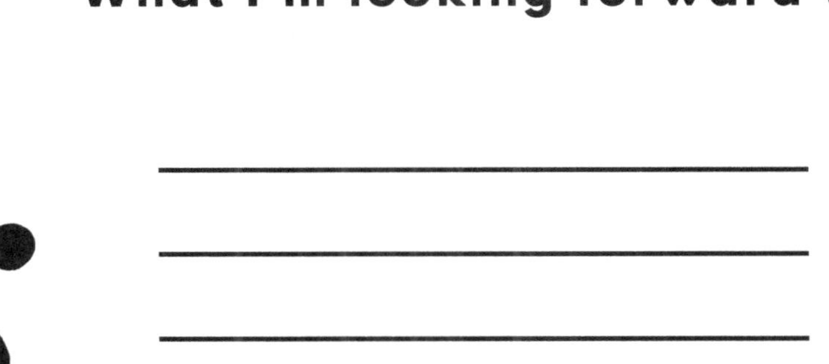

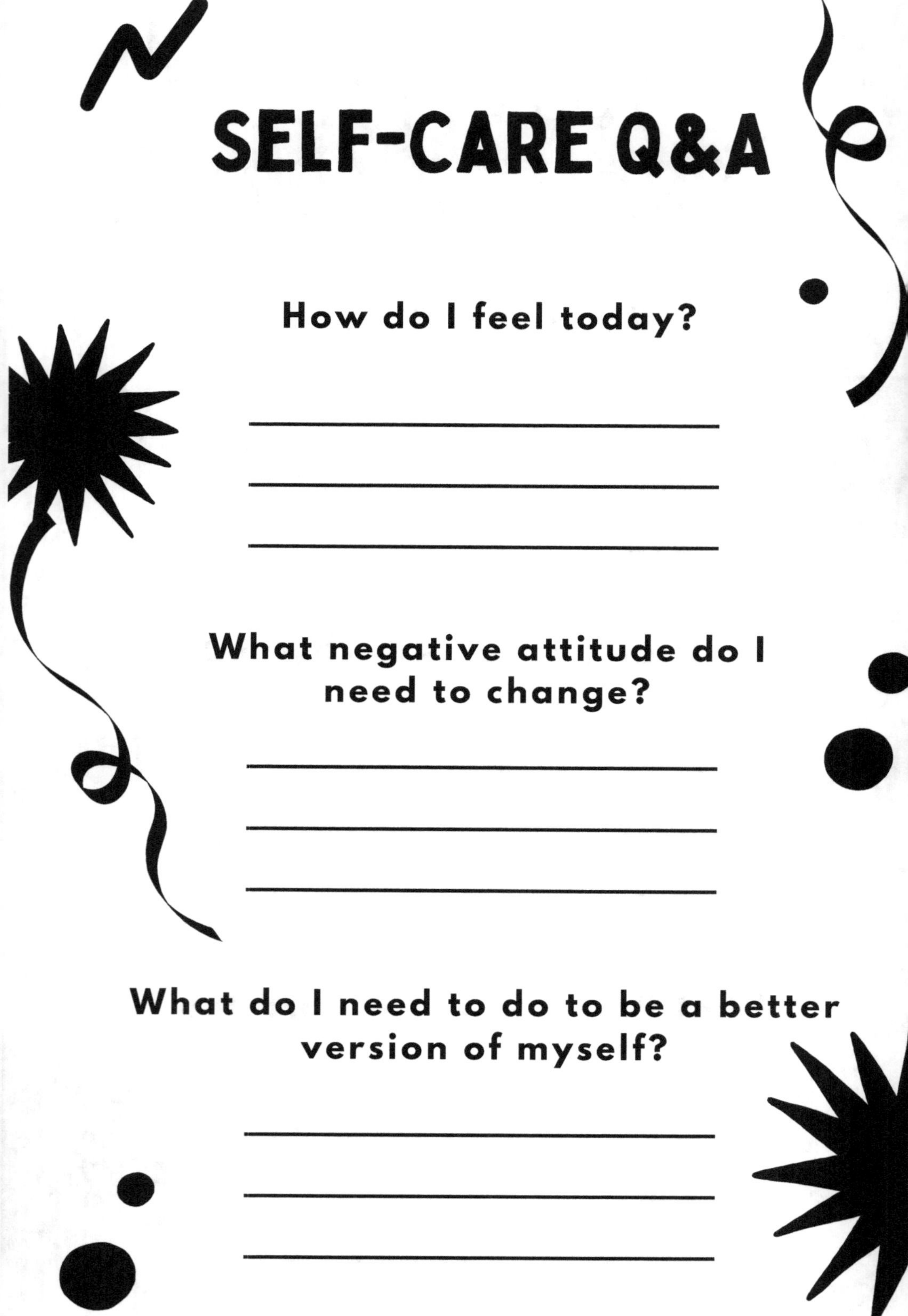

SELF-CARE Q&A

How do I feel today?

What negative attitude do I need to change?

What do I need to do to be a better version of myself?

TODAY I'M GRATEFUL FOR

I'm thankful for:

____

____

____

Goals and dreams I achieved:

____

____

____

What I'm looking forward to:

____

____

____

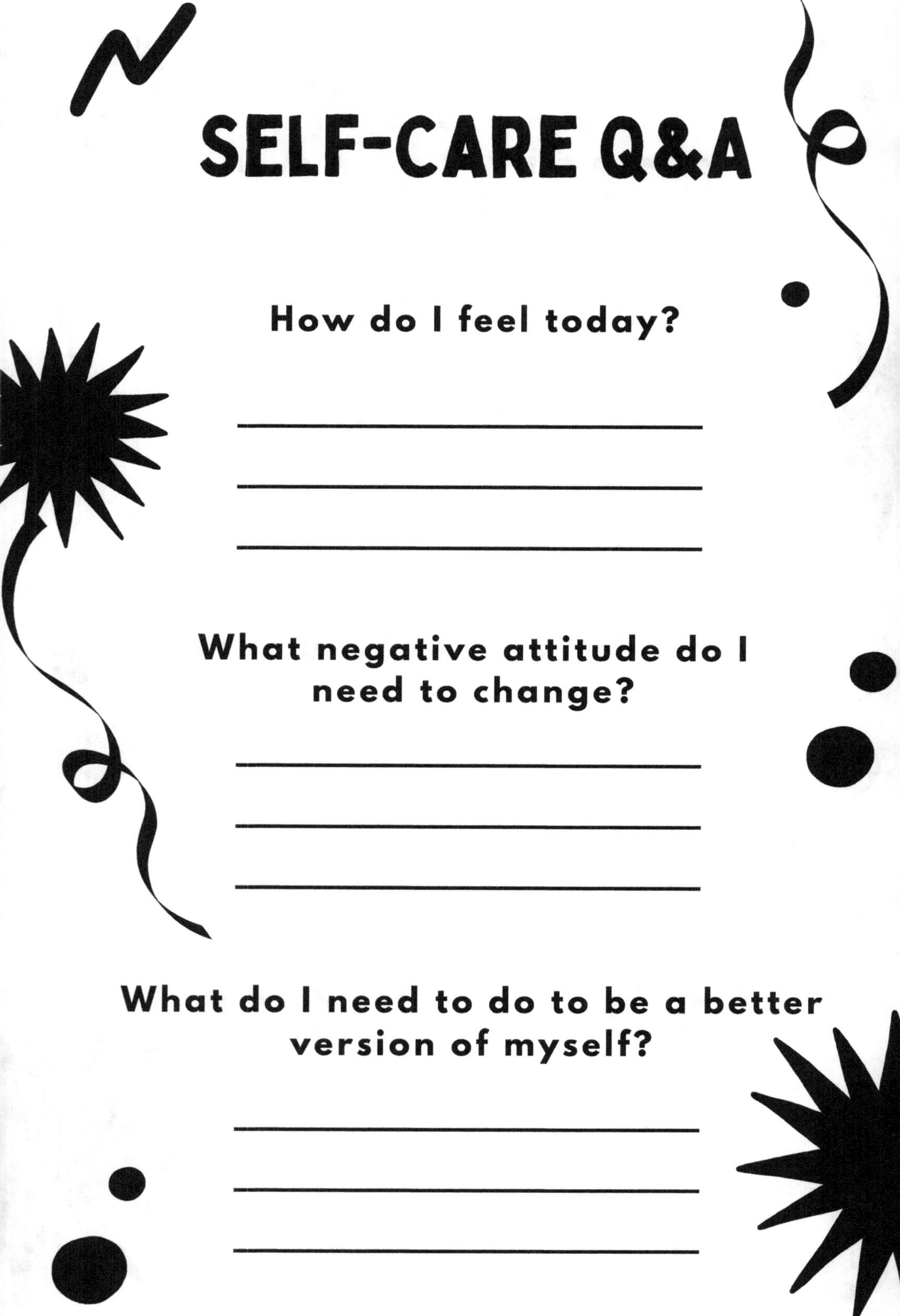

SELF-CARE Q&A
How do I feel today?
What negative attitude do I need to change?
What do I need to do to be a better version of myself?

TODAY I'M GRATEFUL FOR

I'm thankful for:

____

____

____

Goals and dreams I achieved:

____

____

____

What I'm looking forward to:

____

____

____

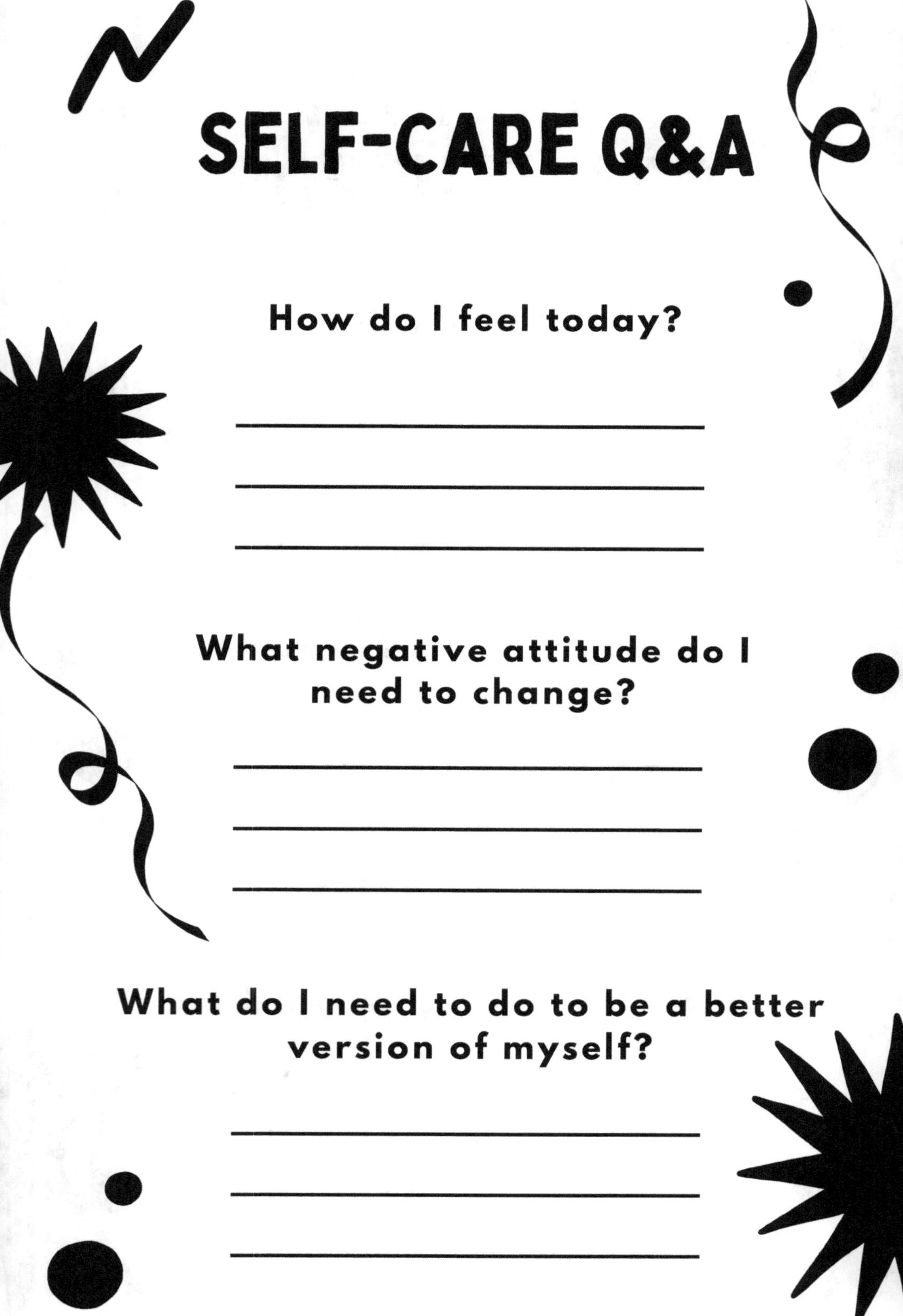

SELF-CARE Q&A

How do I feel today?

What negative attitude do I
need to change?

What do I need to do to be a better
version of myself?

TODAY I'M GRATEFUL FOR

I'm thankful for:

____

____

____

Goals and dreams I achieved:

____

____

____

What I'm looking forward to:

____

____

____

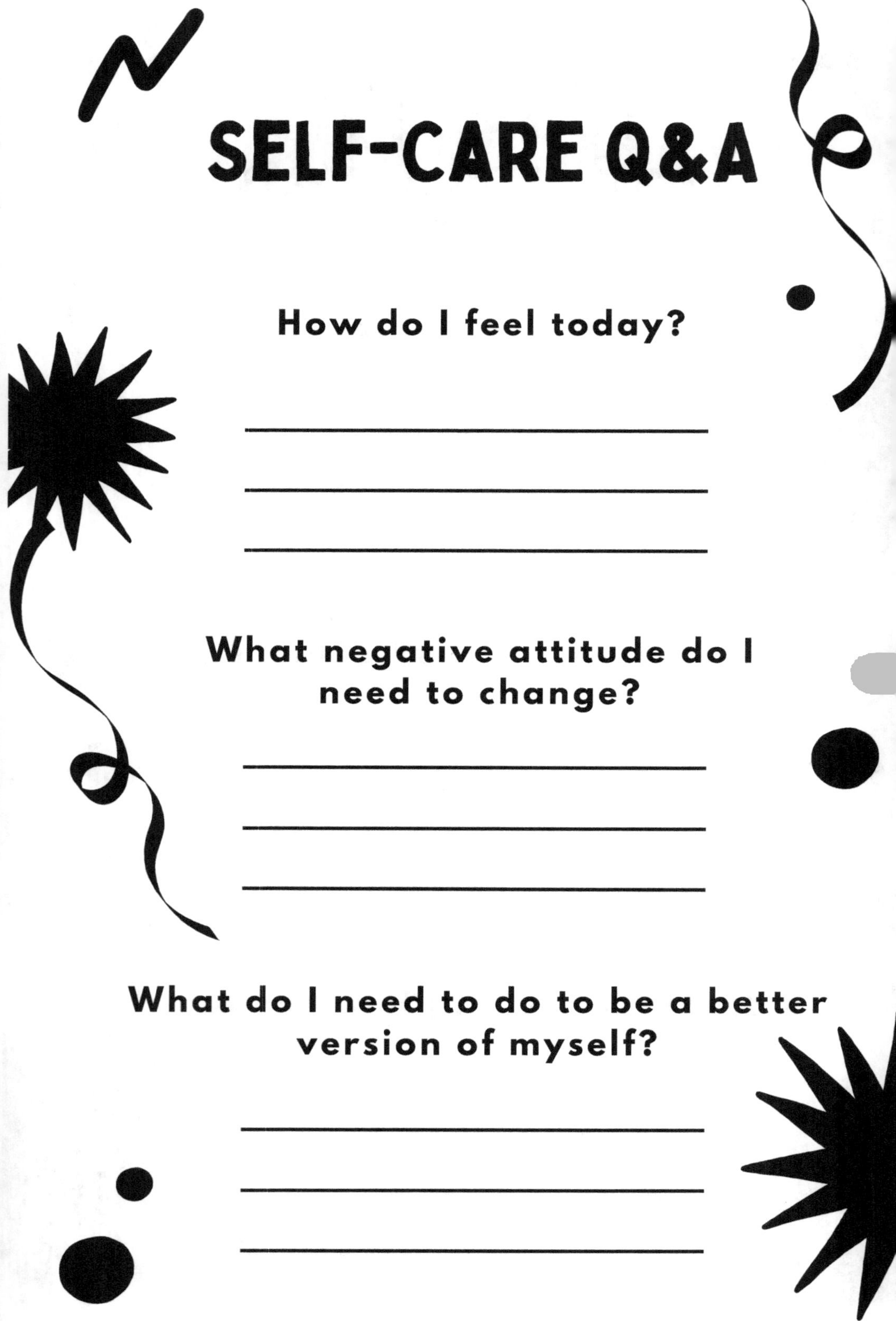

SELF-CARE Q&A

How do I feel today?

What negative attitude do I
need to change?

What do I need to do to be a better
version of myself?

TODAY I'M GRATEFUL FOR

I'm thankful for:

____

____

____

Goals and dreams I achieved:

____

____

____

What I'm looking forward to:

____

____

____

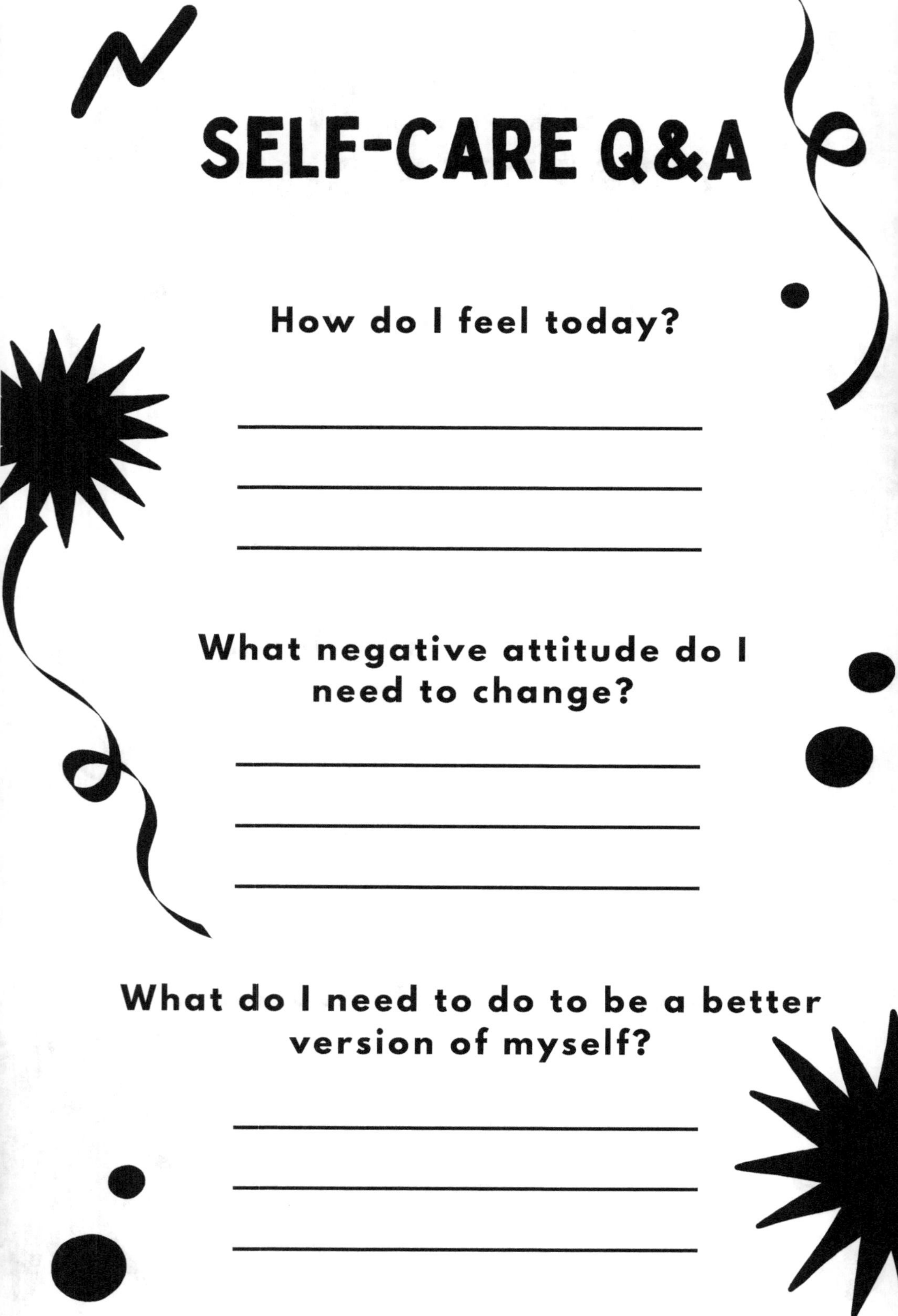

SELF-CARE Q&A

How do I feel today?

What negative attitude do I
need to change?

What do I need to do to be a better
version of myself?

TODAY I'M GRATEFUL FOR

I'm thankful for:

____

____

____

Goals and dreams I achieved:

____

____

____

What I'm looking forward to:

____

____

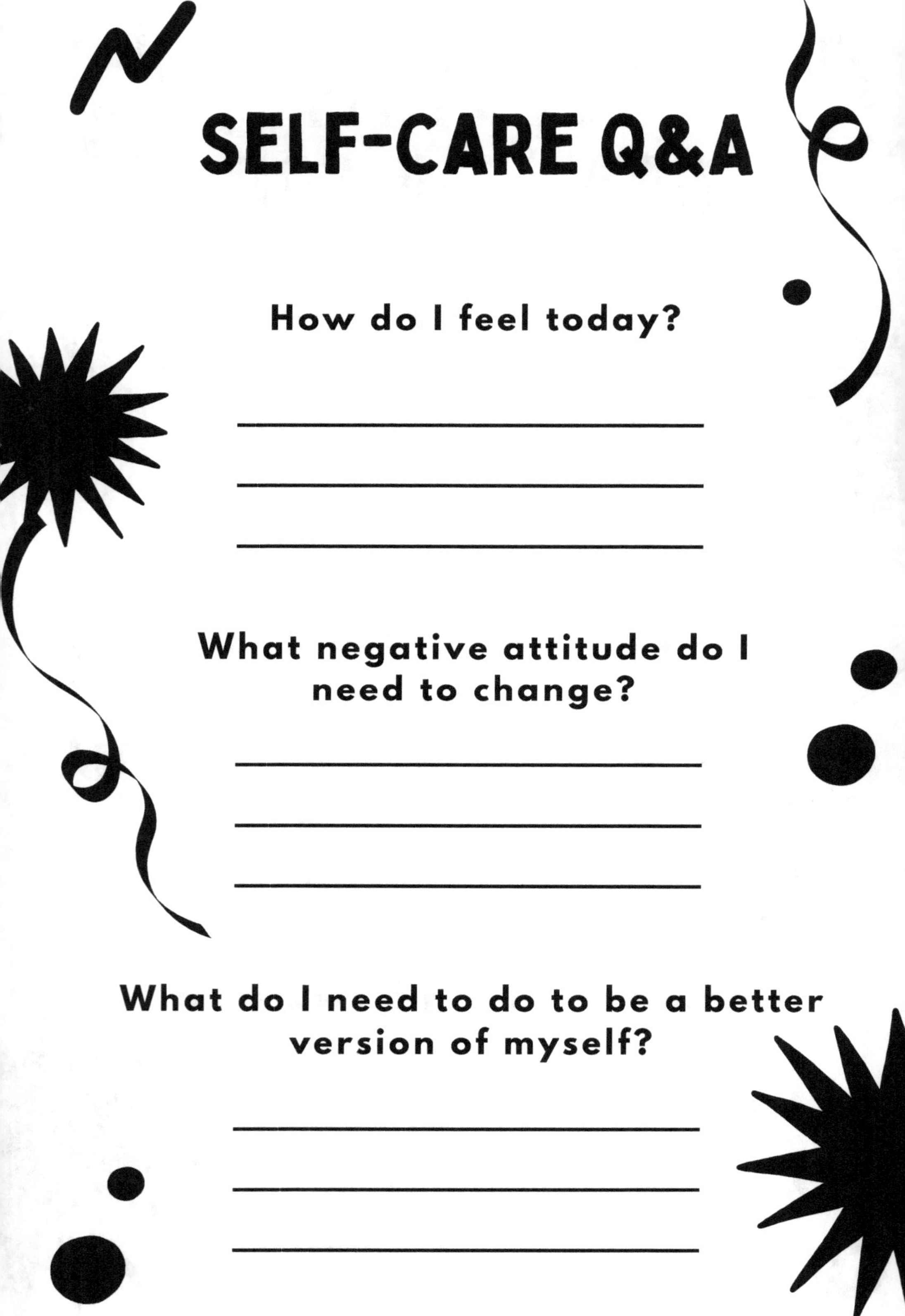

SELF-CARE Q&A

How do I feel today?

____

____

____

What negative attitude do I need to change?

____

____

____

What do I need to do to be a better version of myself?

____

____

____

TODAY I'M GRATEFUL FOR

I'm thankful for:

Goals and dreams I achieved:

What I'm looking forward to:

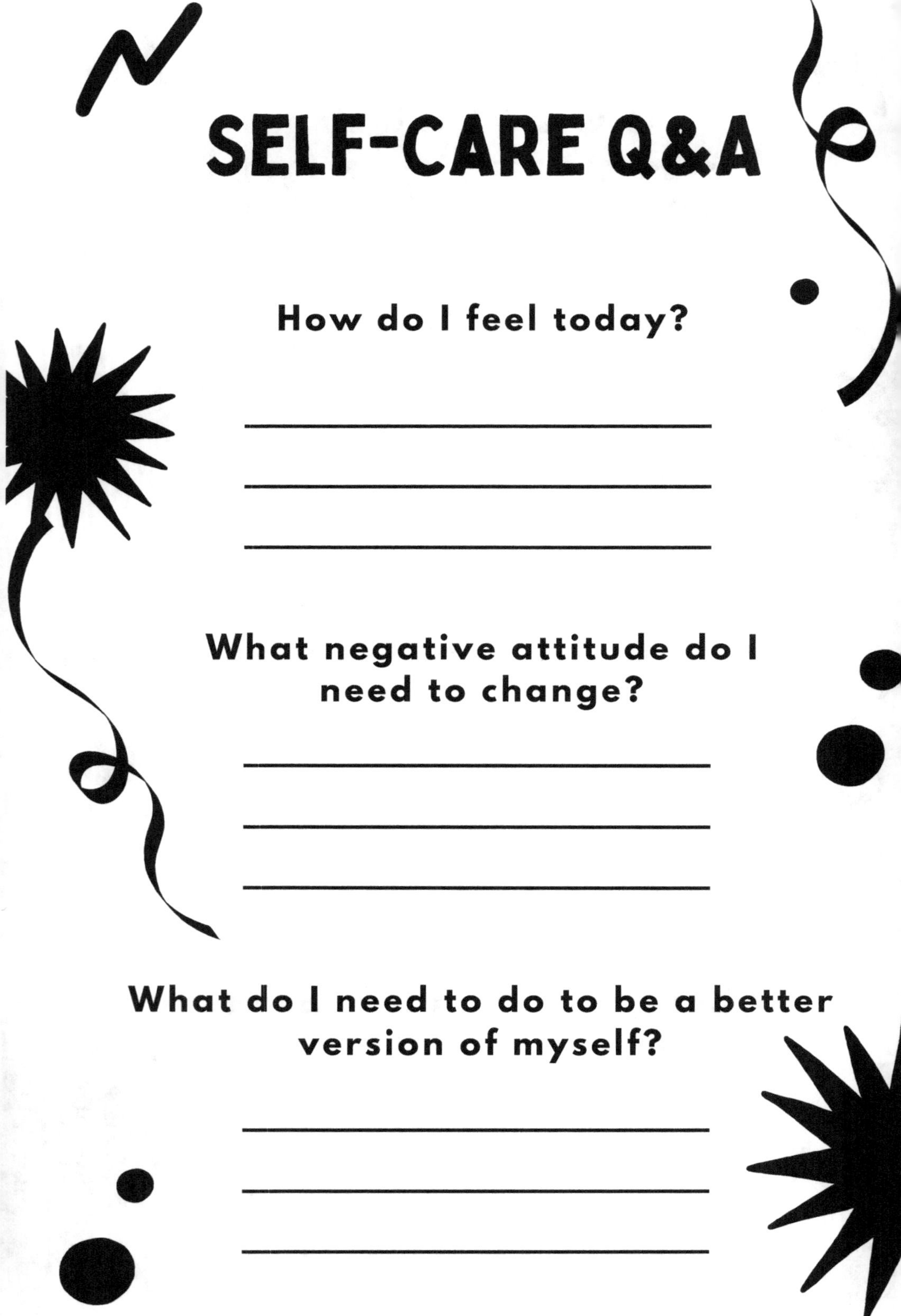

SELF-CARE Q&A

How do I feel today?

What negative attitude do I need to change?

What do I need to do to be a better version of myself?

TODAY I'M GRATEFUL FOR

I'm thankful for:

____

____

____

Goals and dreams I achieved:

____

____

____

What I'm looking forward to:

____

____

____

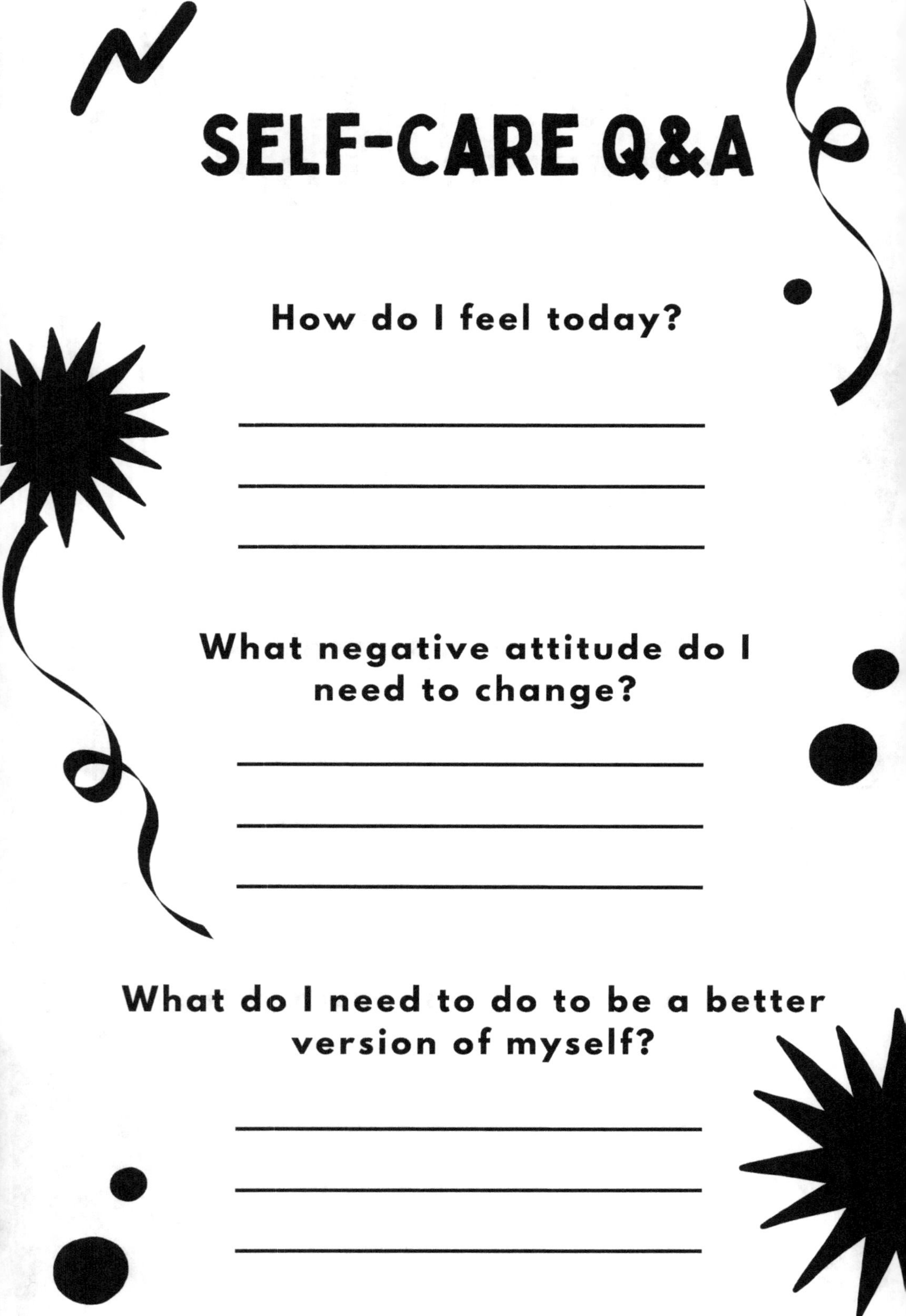

SELF-CARE Q&A

How do I feel today?

____

____

____

What negative attitude do I need to change?

____

____

____

What do I need to do to be a better version of myself?

____

____

TODAY I'M GRATEFUL FOR

I'm thankful for:

Goals and dreams I achieved:

What I'm looking forward to:

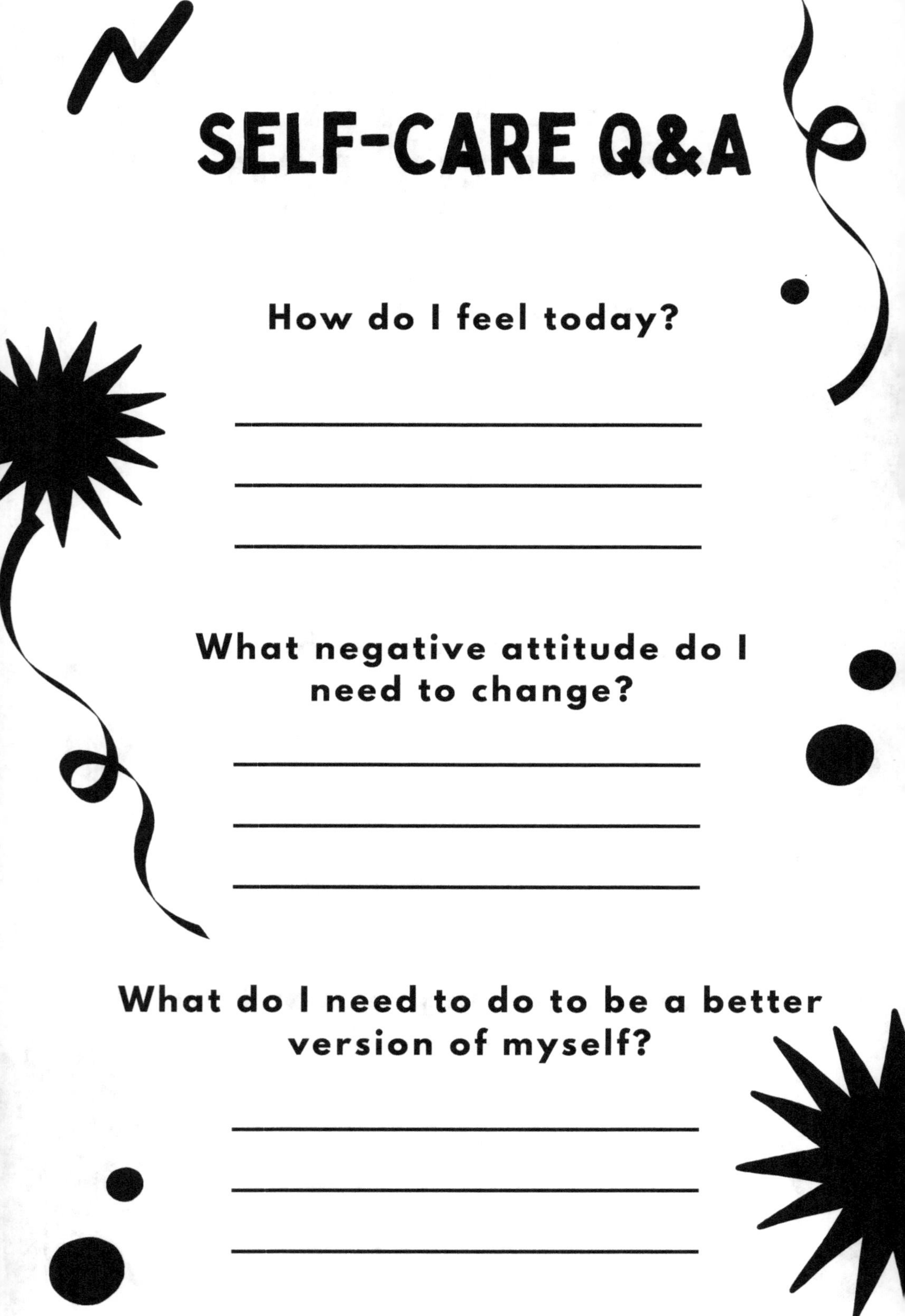

SELF-CARE Q&A

How do I feel today?

____

____

____

What negative attitude do I need to change?

____

____

____

What do I need to do to be a better version of myself?

____

____

____

TODAY I'M
GRATEFUL FOR

I'm thankful for:

Goals and dreams I achieved:

What I'm looking forward to:

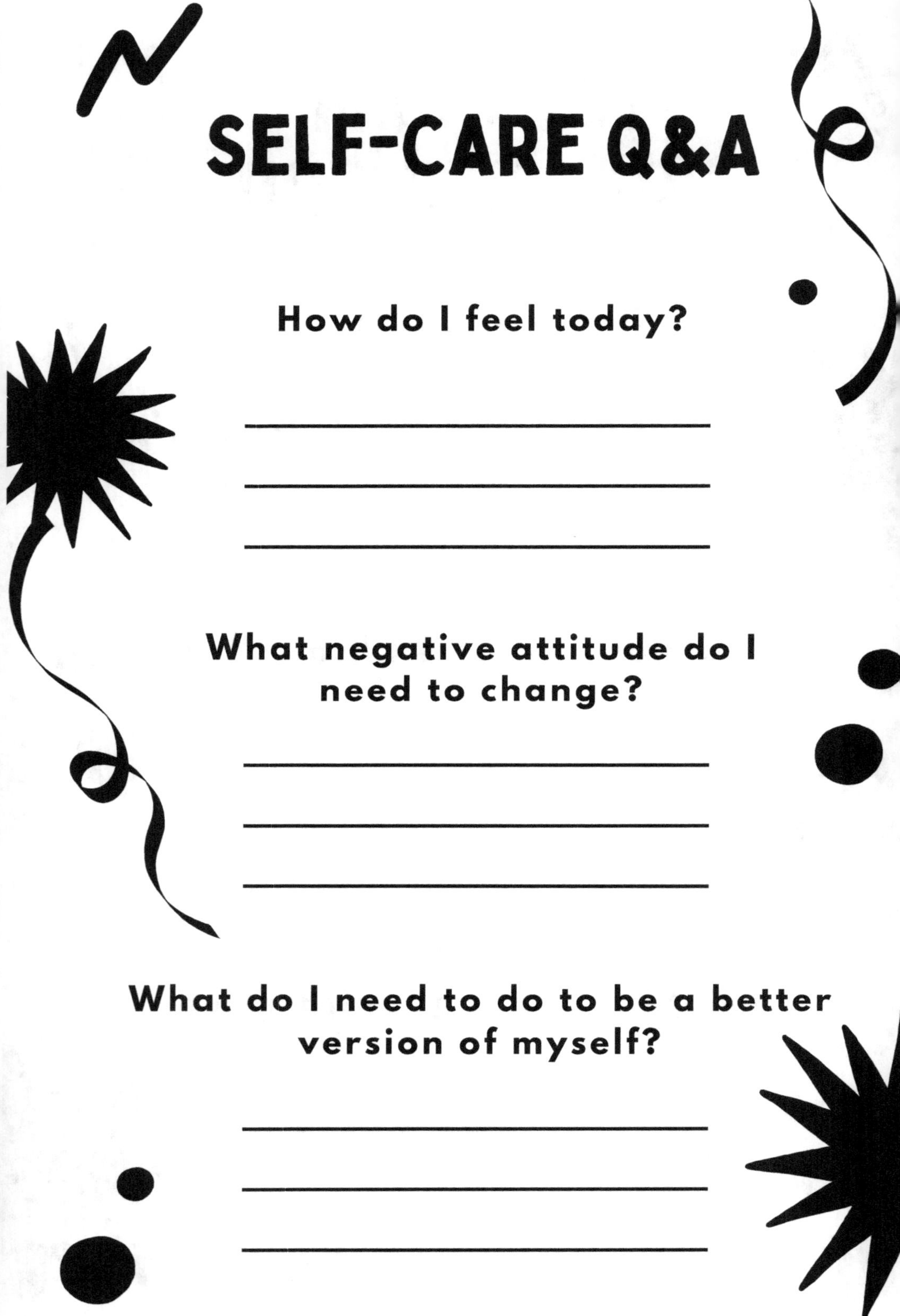

SELF-CARE Q&A

How do I feel today?

____

____

____

What negative attitude do I need to change?

____

____

____

What do I need to do to be a better version of myself?

____

____

____

TODAY I'M GRATEFUL FOR

I'm thankful for:

____

____

____

Goals and dreams I achieved:

____

____

____

What I'm looking forward to:

____

____

____

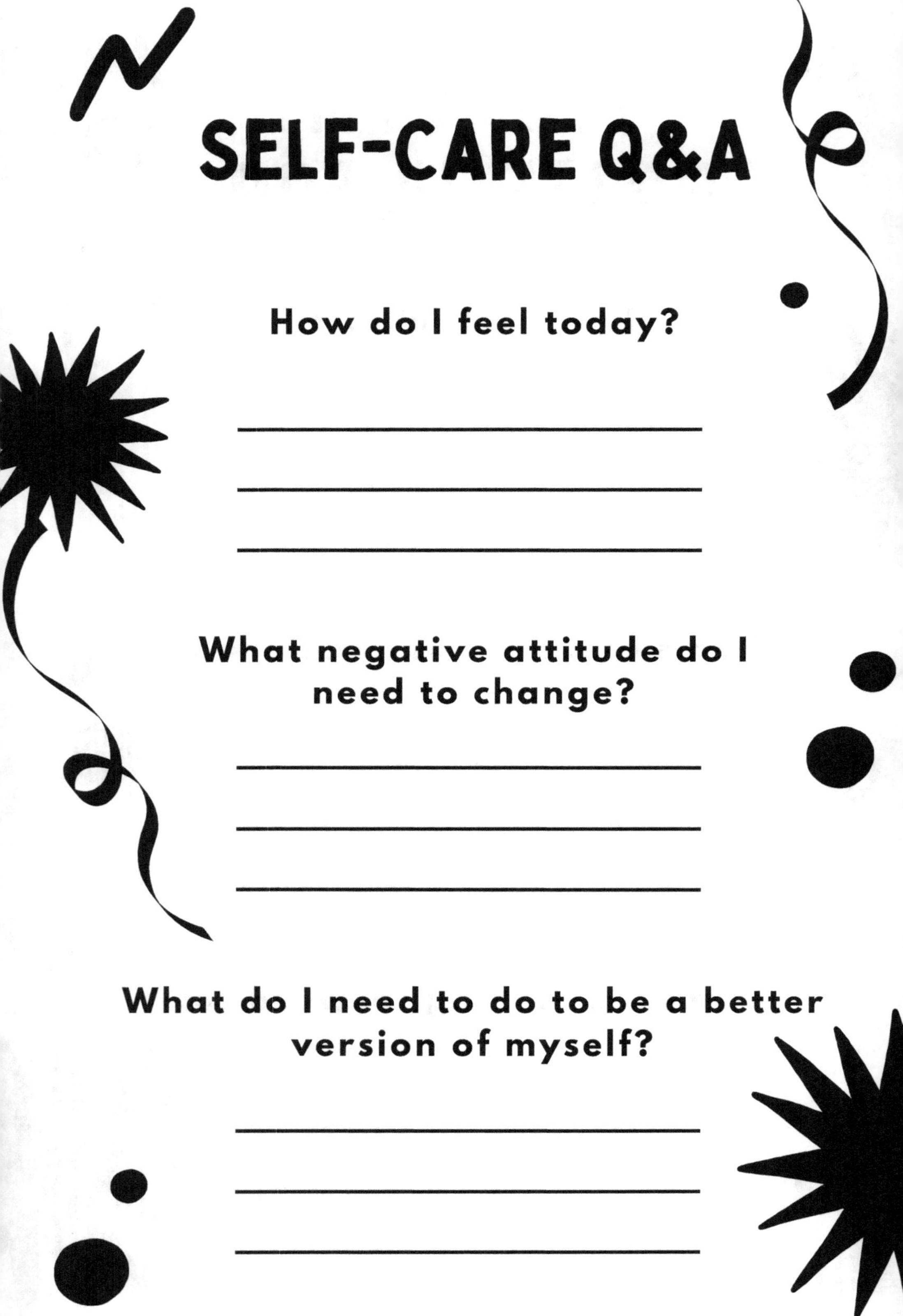

SELF-CARE Q&A

How do I feel today?

What negative attitude do I
need to change?

What do I need to do to be a better
version of myself?

TODAY I'M GRATEFUL FOR

I'm thankful for:

____

____

____

Goals and dreams I achieved:

____

____

____

What I'm looking forward to:

____

____

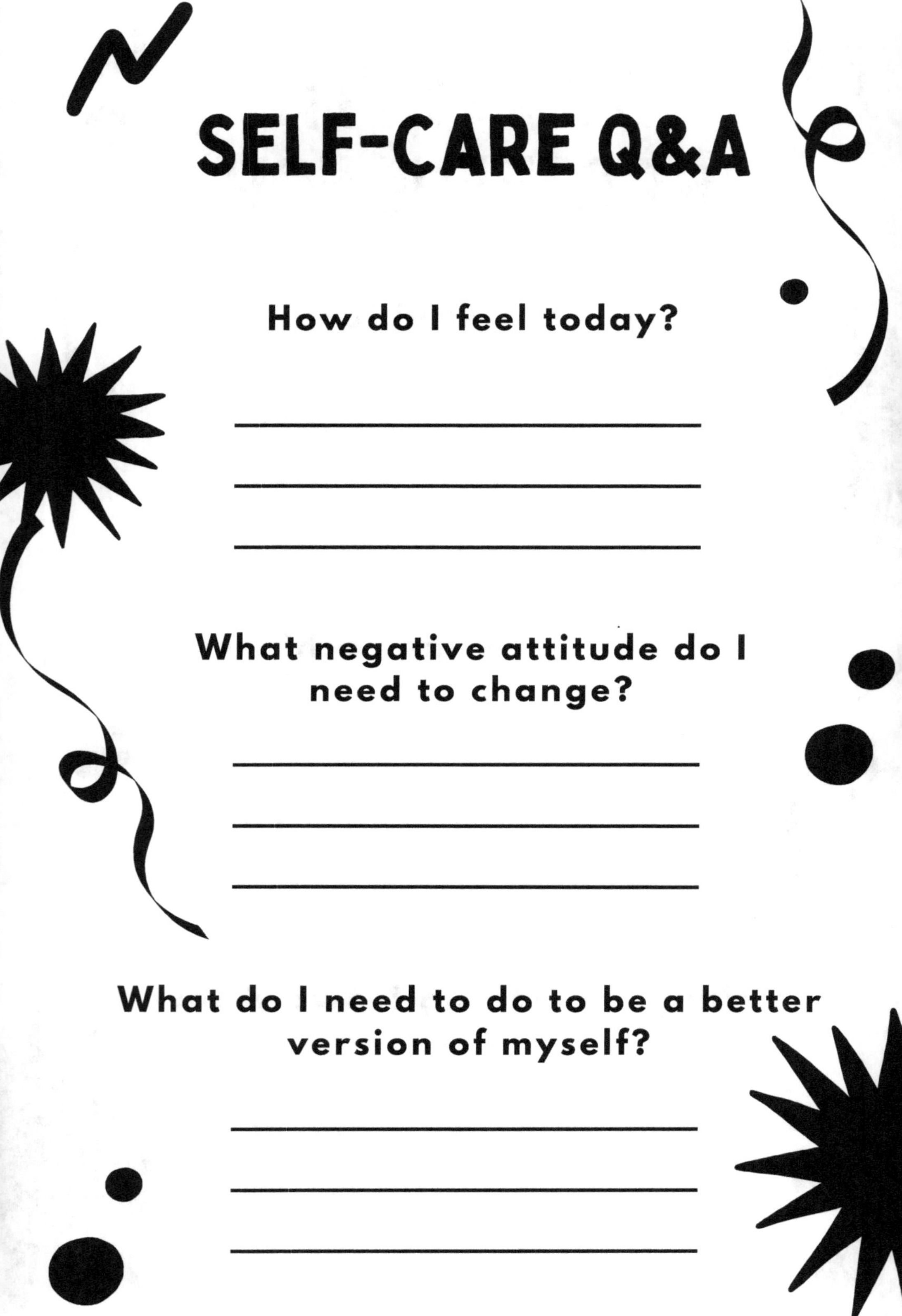

SELF-CARE Q&A

How do I feel today?

What negative attitude do I
need to change?

What do I need to do to be a better
version of myself?

TODAY I'M GRATEFUL FOR

I'm thankful for:

____

____

____

Goals and dreams I achieved:

____

____

____

What I'm looking forward to:

____

____

____

SELF-CARE Q&A

How do I feel today?

What negative attitude do I
need to change?

What do I need to do to be a better
version of myself?

TODAY I'M GRATEFUL FOR

I'm thankful for:

____

____

____

Goals and dreams I achieved:

____

____

____

What I'm looking forward to:

____

____

____

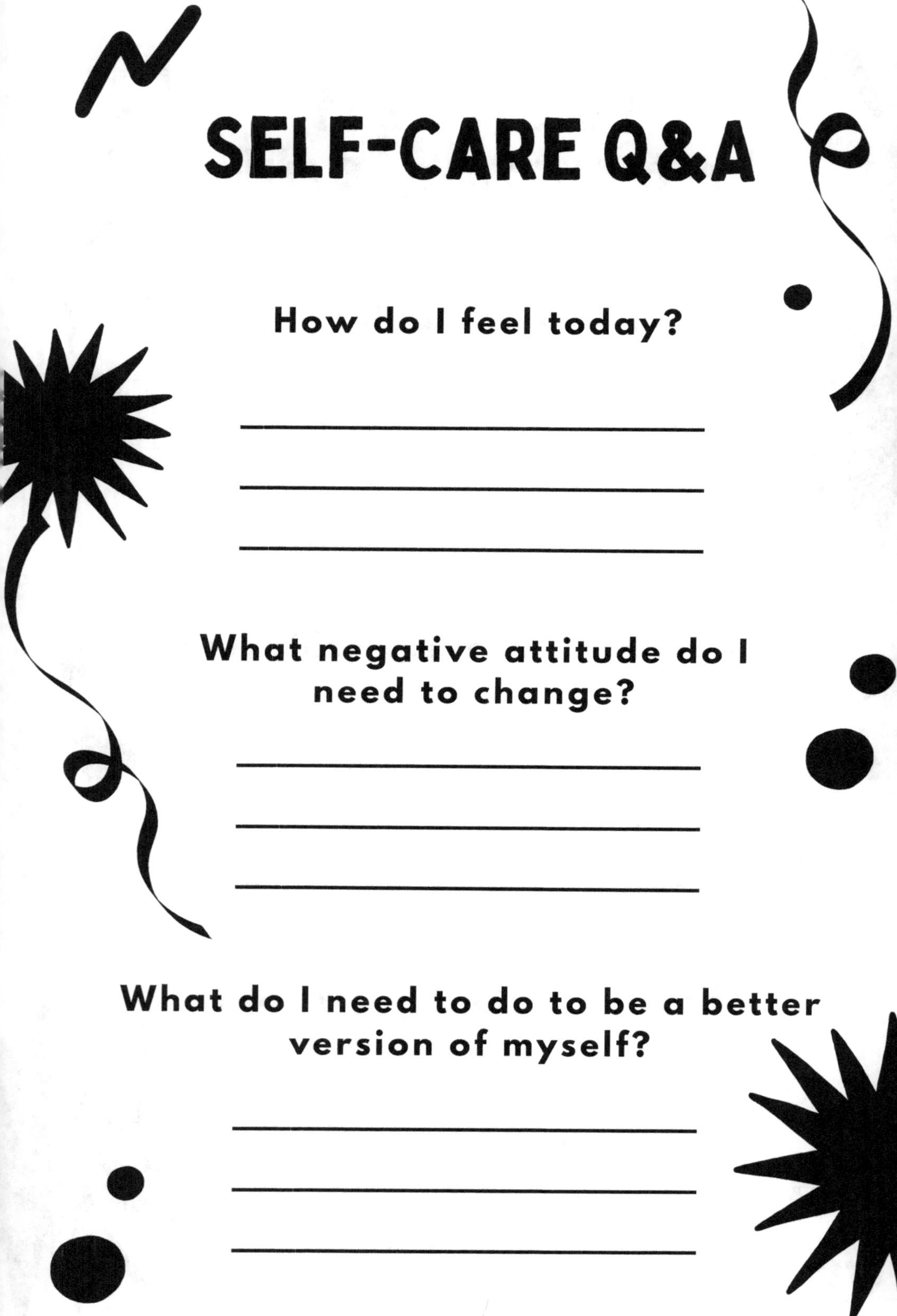

SELF-CARE Q&A

How do I feel today?

What negative attitude do I
need to change?

What do I need to do to be a better
version of myself?

TODAY I'M GRATEFUL FOR

I'm thankful for:

____

____

____

Goals and dreams I achieved:

____

____

____

What I'm looking forward to:

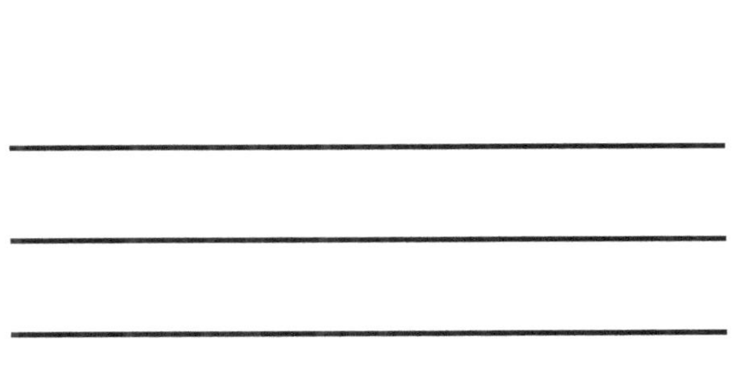

____

____

____

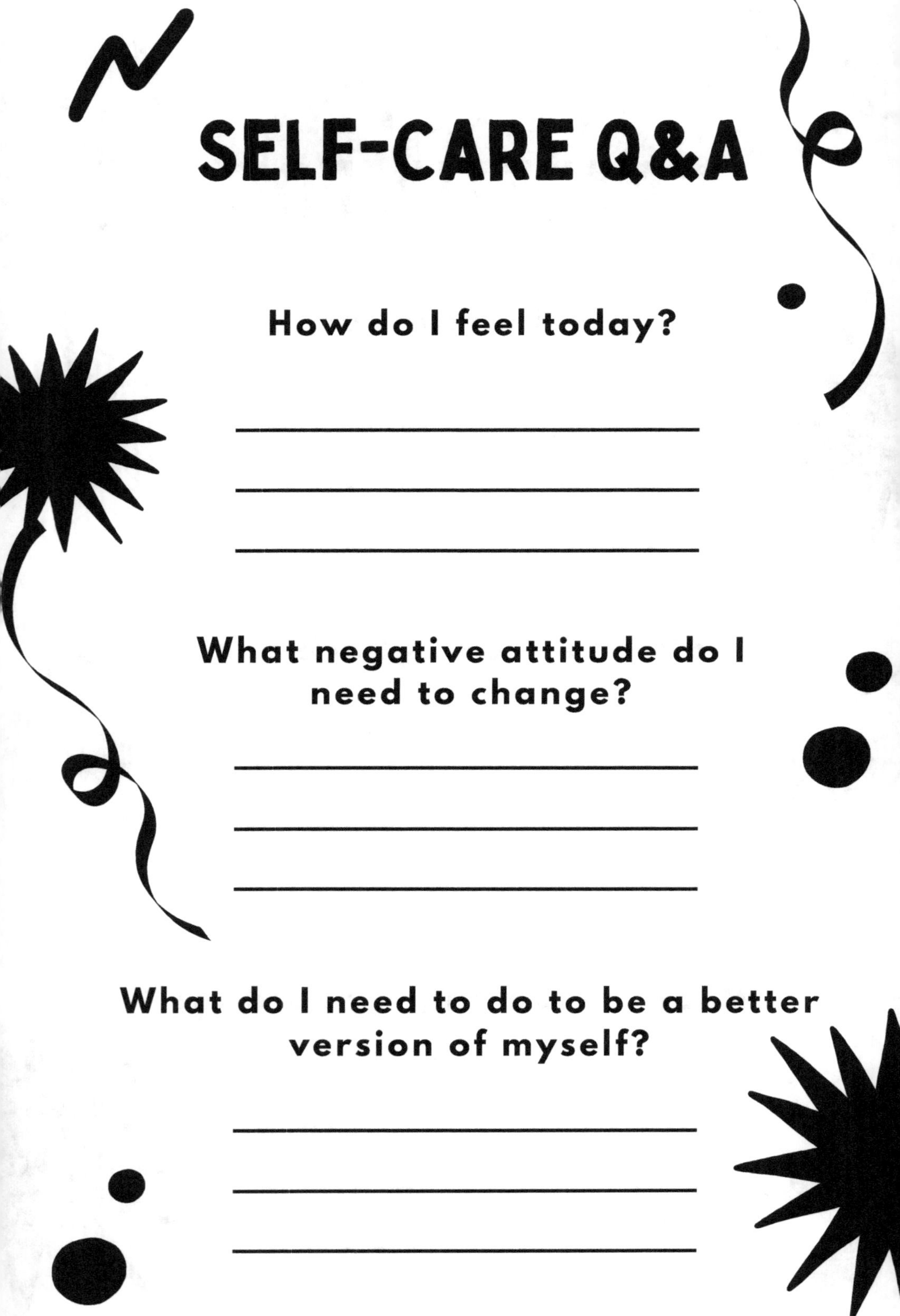

SELF-CARE Q&A

How do I feel today?

What negative attitude do I
need to change?

What do I need to do to be a better
version of myself?

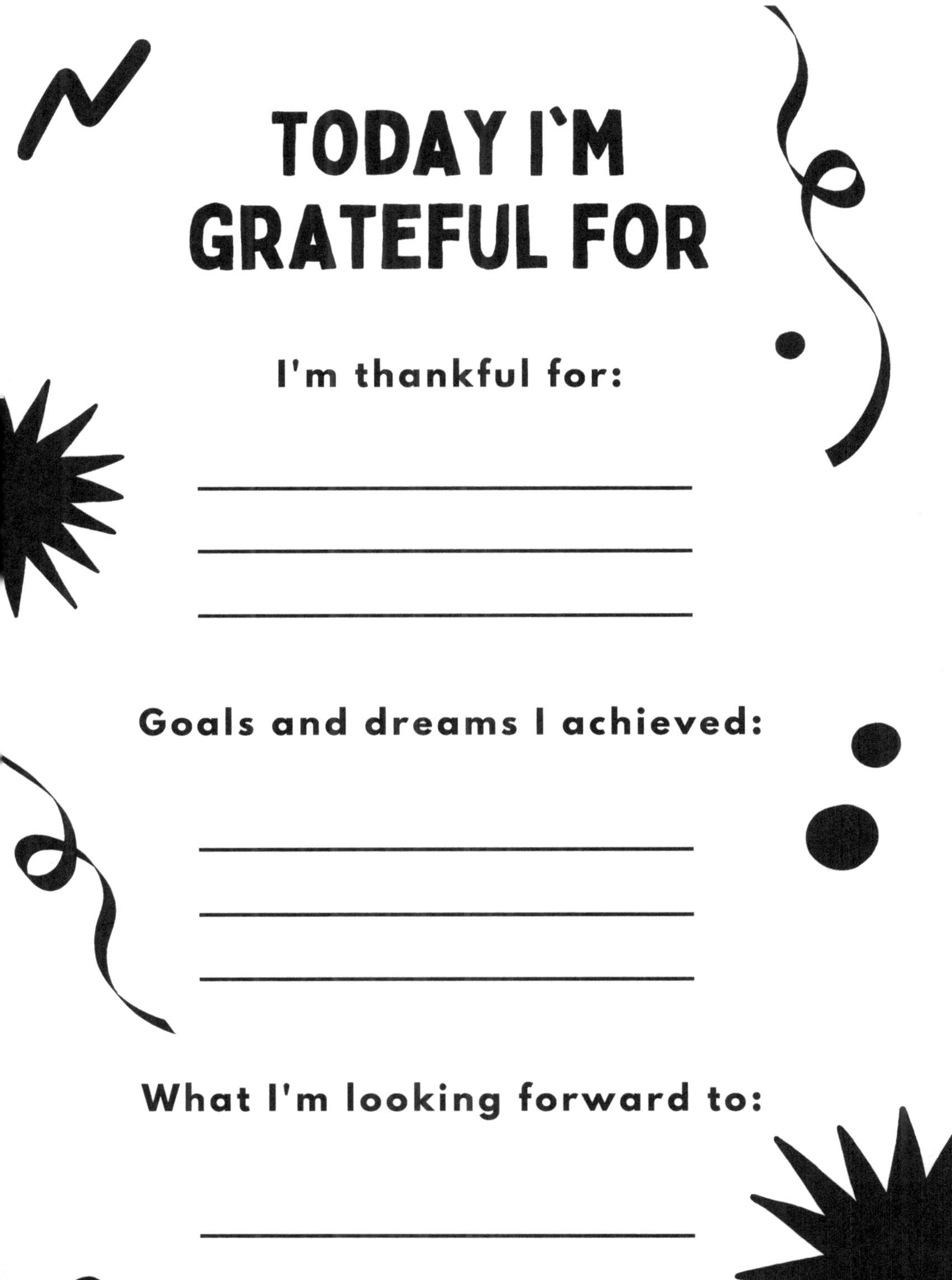

TODAY I'M GRATEFUL FOR
I'm thankful for:
Goals and dreams I achieved:
What I'm looking forward to:

SELF-CARE Q&A

How do I feel today?

What negative attitude do I need to change?

What do I need to do to be a better version of myself?

TODAY I'M GRATEFUL FOR

I'm thankful for:

____

____

____

Goals and dreams I achieved:

____

____

____

What I'm looking forward to:

____

____

____

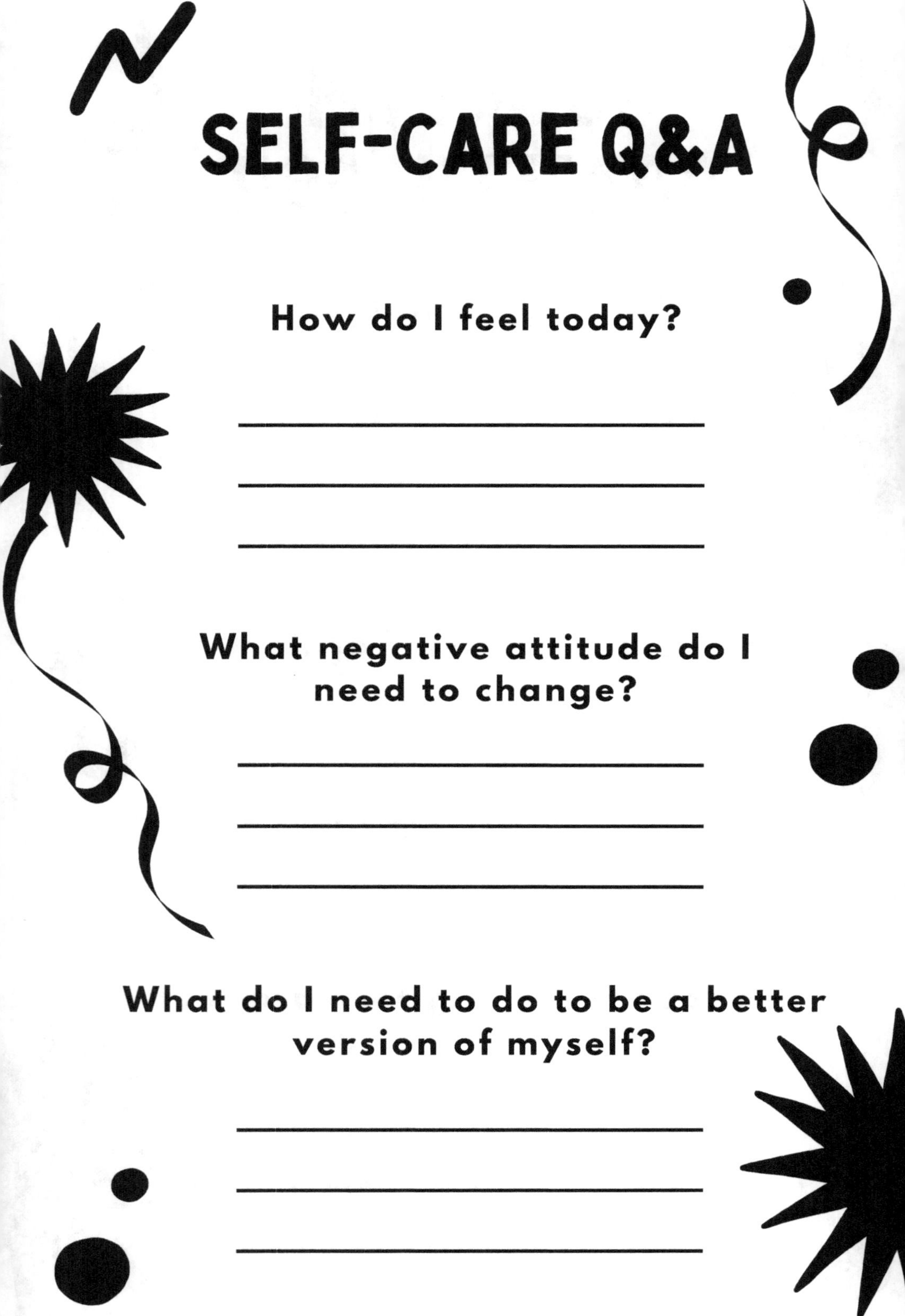

SELF-CARE Q&A

How do I feel today?

What negative attitude do I
need to change?

What do I need to do to be a better
version of myself?

TODAY I'M GRATEFUL FOR

I'm thankful for:

____

____

____

Goals and dreams I achieved:

____

____

____

What I'm looking forward to:

____

____

____

SELF-CARE Q&A

How do I feel today?

____

____

____

**What negative attitude do I
need to change?**

____

____

____

**What do I need to do to be a better
version of myself?**

____

____

____

TODAY I'M GRATEFUL FOR

I'm thankful for:

____

____

____

Goals and dreams I achieved:

____

____

____

What I'm looking forward to:

____

____

____

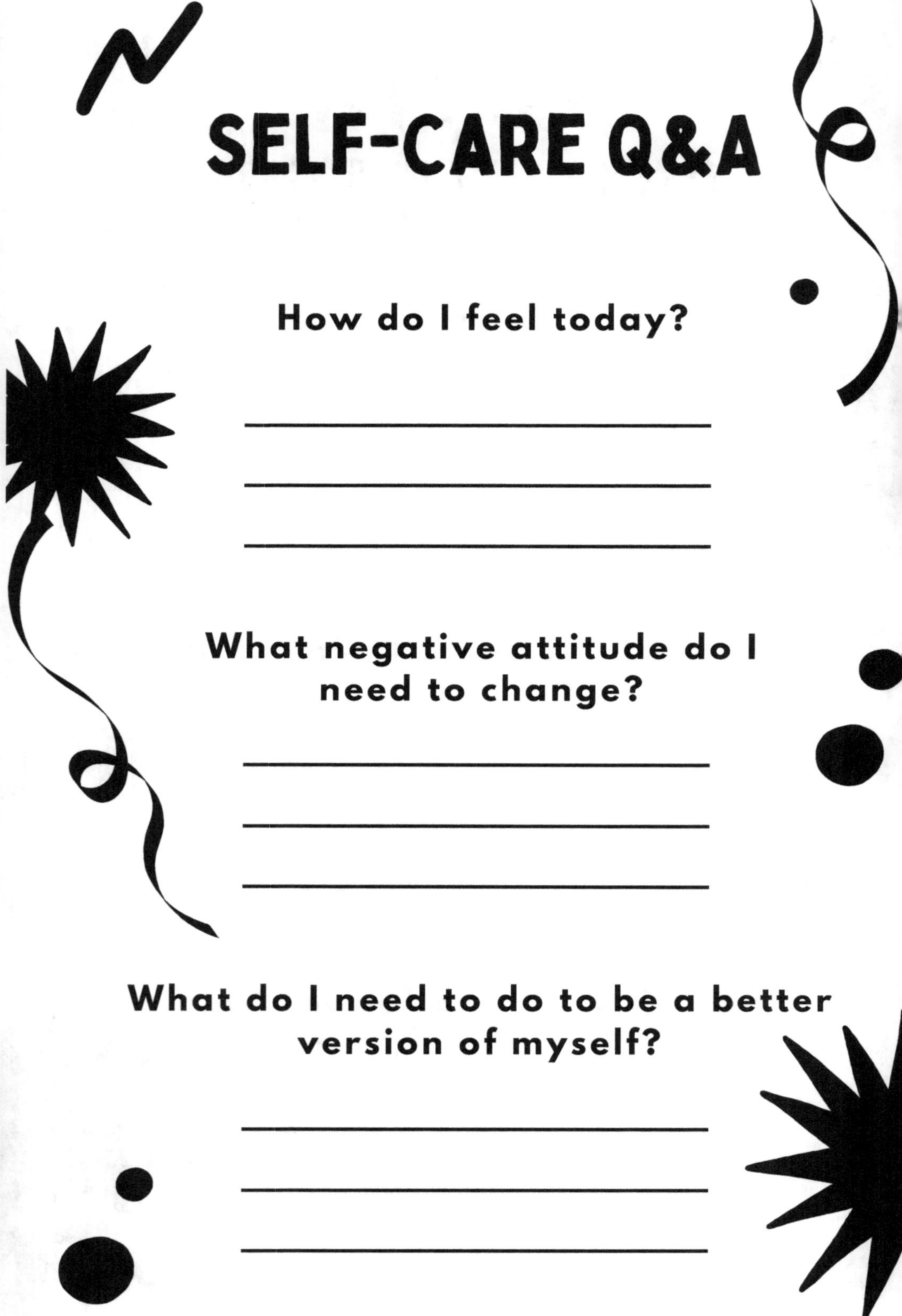

SELF-CARE Q&A

How do I feel today?

____

____

____

What negative attitude do I need to change?

____

____

____

What do I need to do to be a better version of myself?

____

____

____

TODAY I'M GRATEFUL FOR

I'm thankful for:

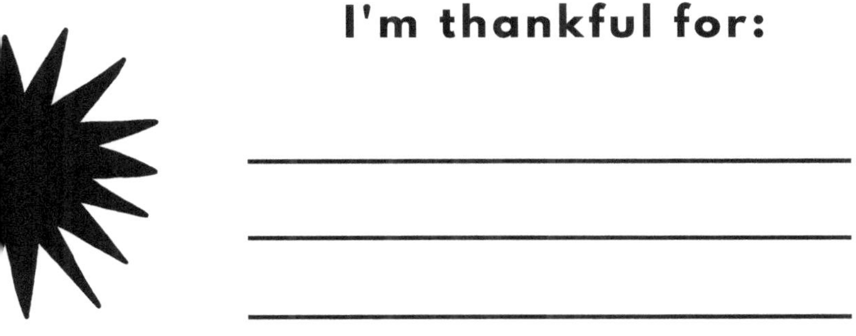

Goals and dreams I achieved:

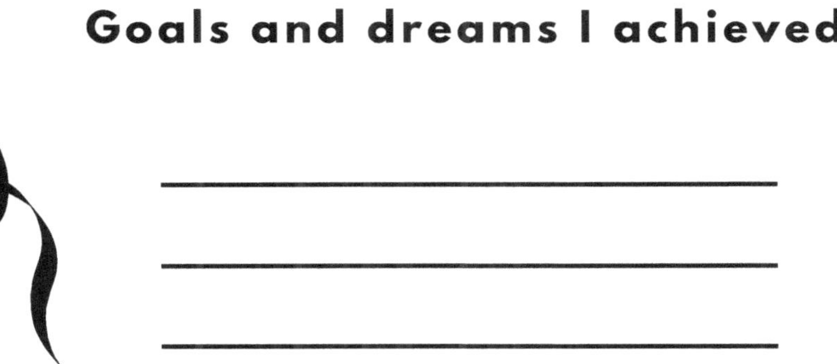

What I'm looking forward to:

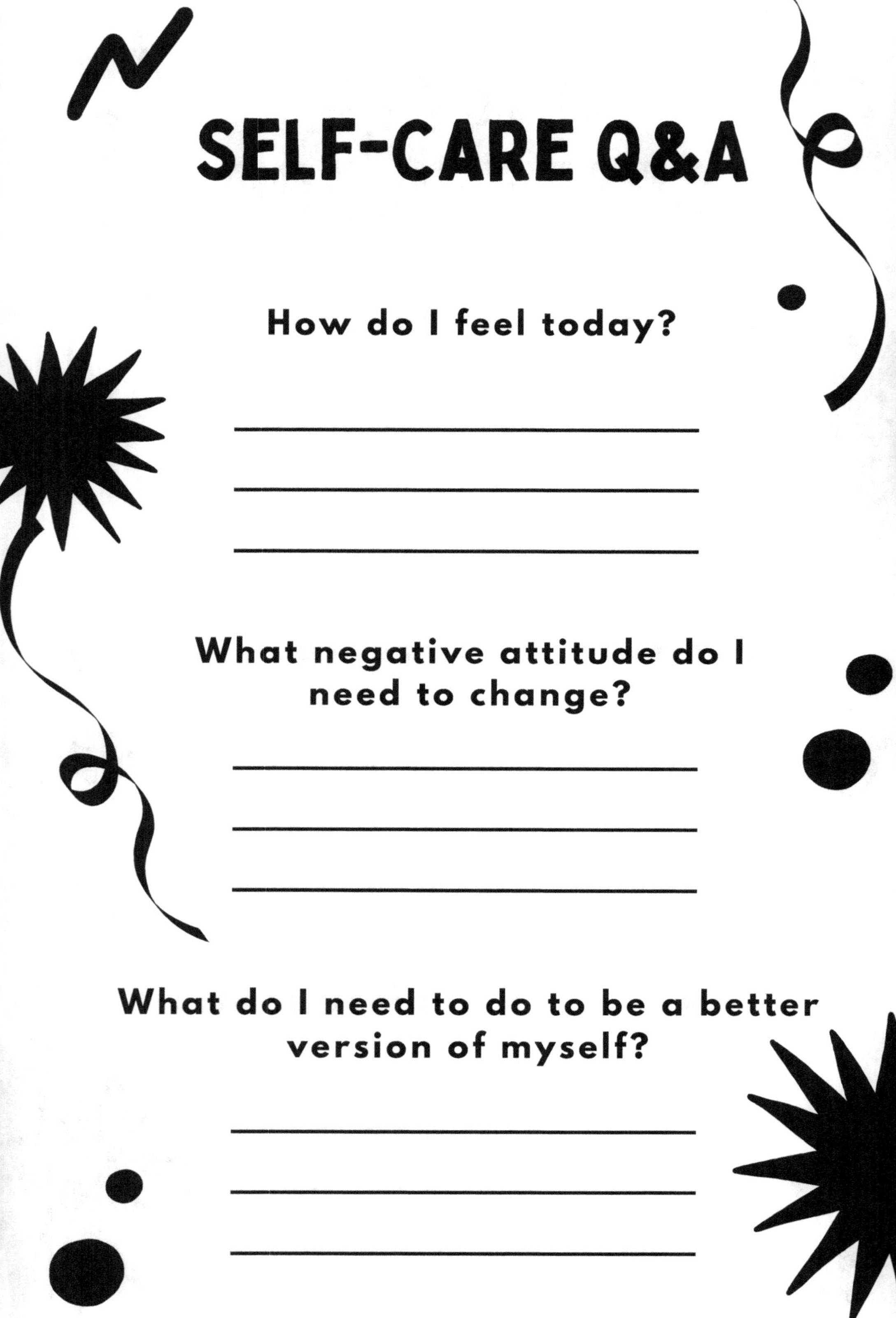

SELF-CARE Q&A

How do I feel today?

**What negative attitude do I
need to change?**

**What do I need to do to be a better
version of myself?**

TODAY I'M GRATEFUL FOR

I'm thankful for:

____

____

____

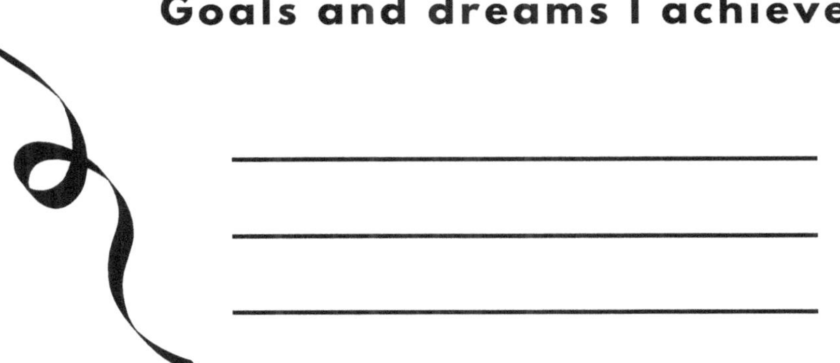

Goals and dreams I achieved:

____

____

____

What I'm looking forward to:

____

____

____

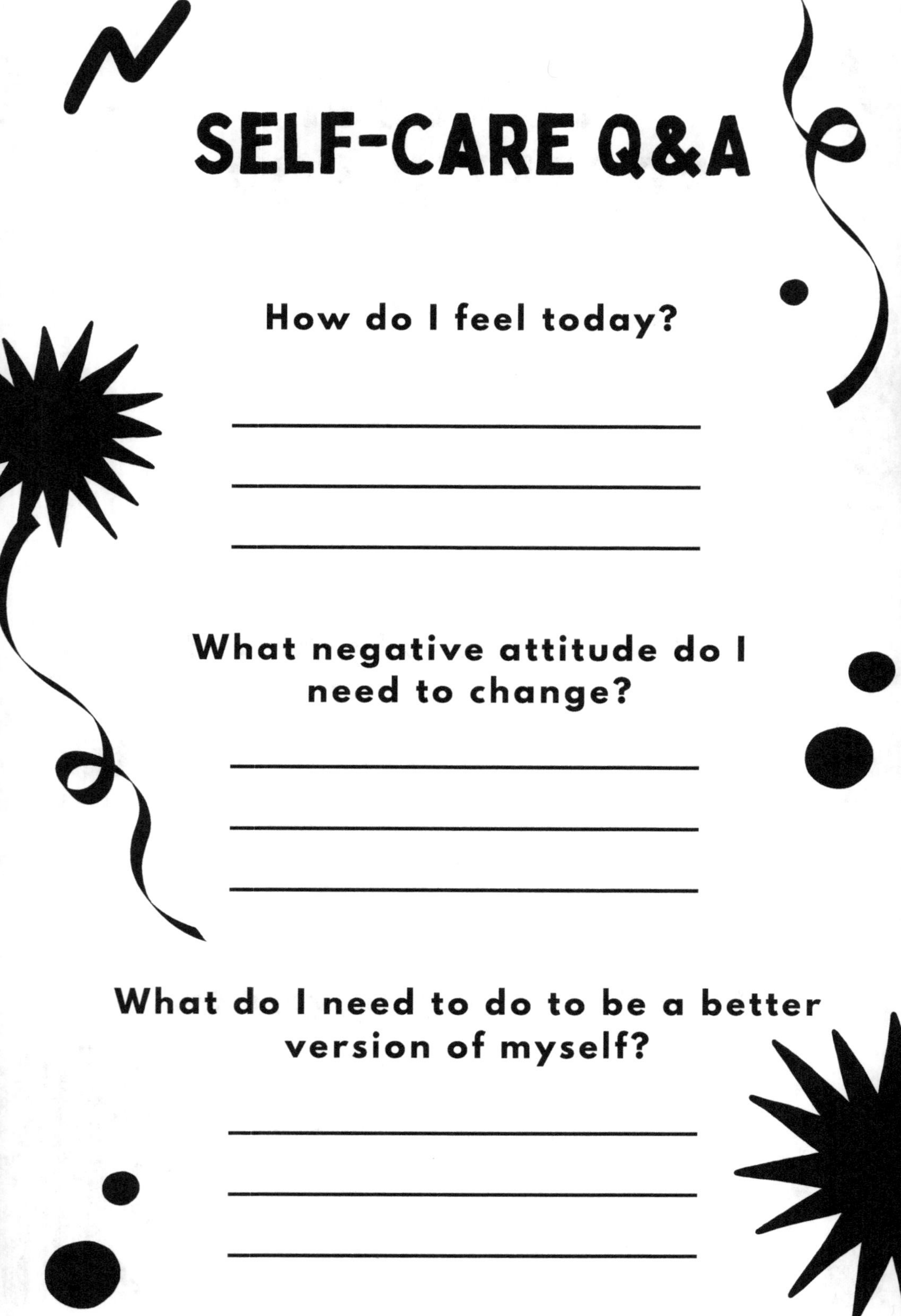

SELF-CARE Q&A

How do I feel today?

____

____

____

What negative attitude do I
need to change?

____

____

____

What do I need to do to be a better
version of myself?

____

____

TODAY I'M GRATEFUL FOR

I'm thankful for:

____

____

____

Goals and dreams I achieved:

____

____

____

What I'm looking forward to:

____

____

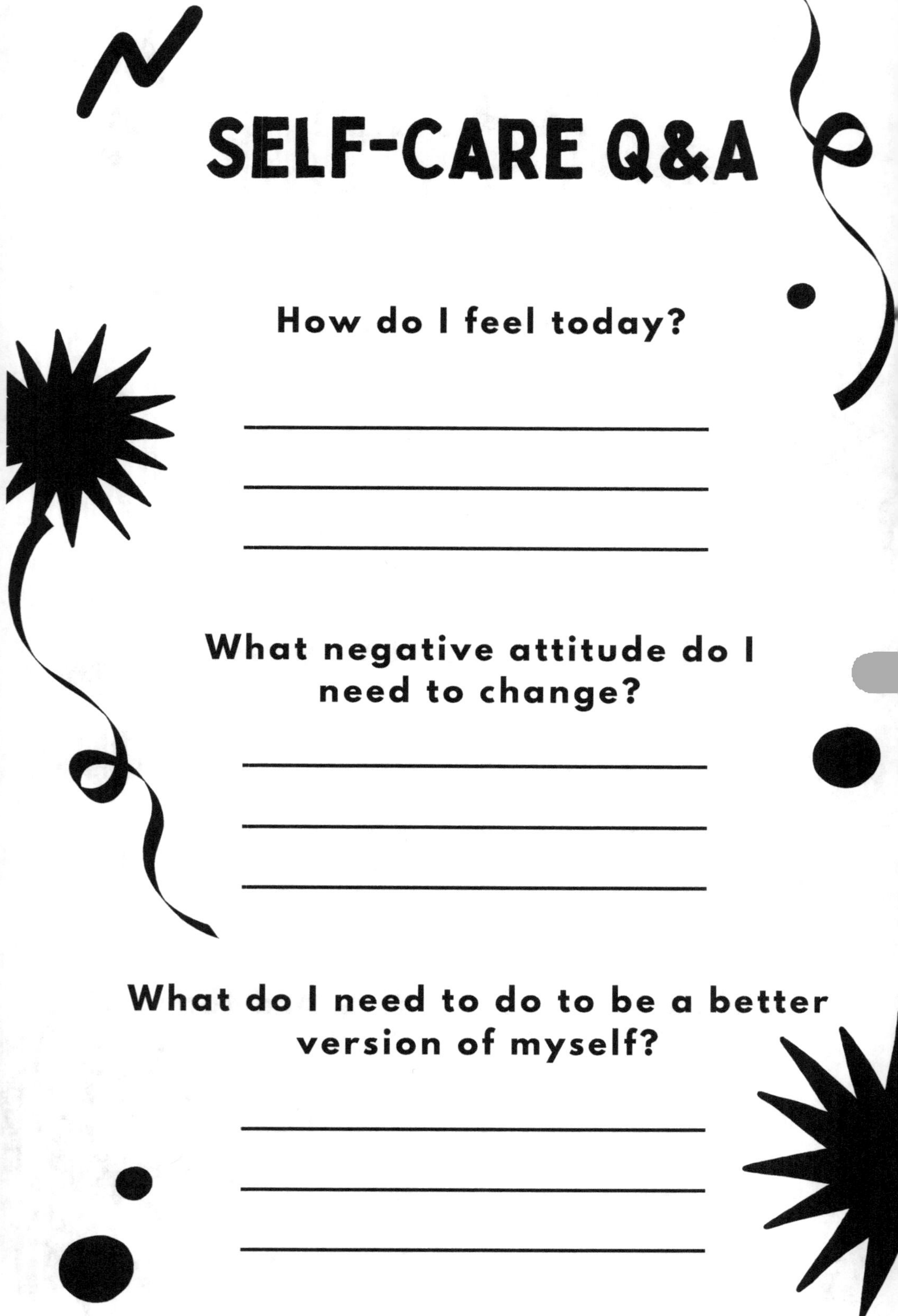

SELF-CARE Q&A

How do I feel today?

What negative attitude do I
need to change?

What do I need to do to be a better
version of myself?

TODAY I'M GRATEFUL FOR

I'm thankful for:

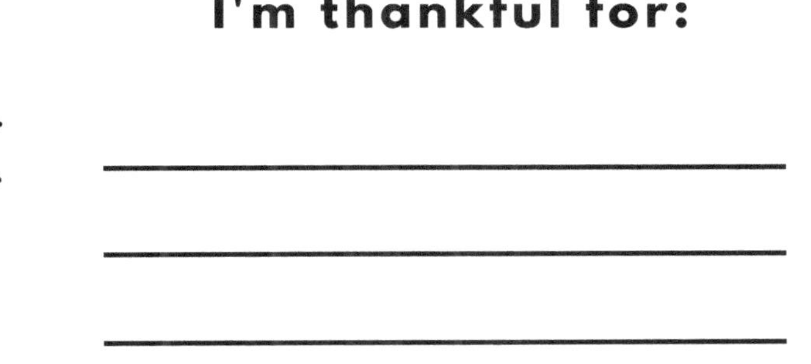

Goals and dreams I achieved:

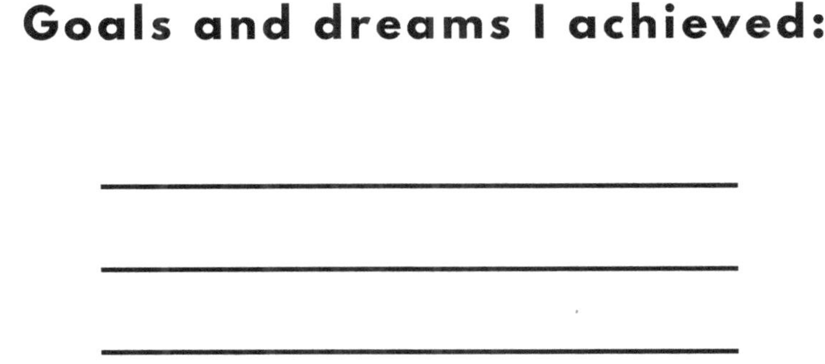

What I'm looking forward to:

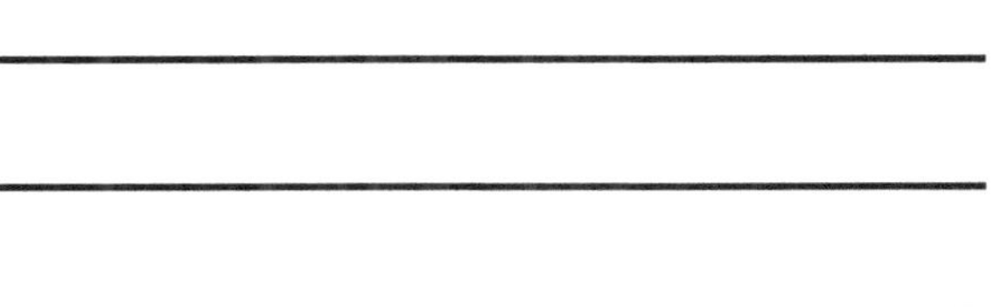

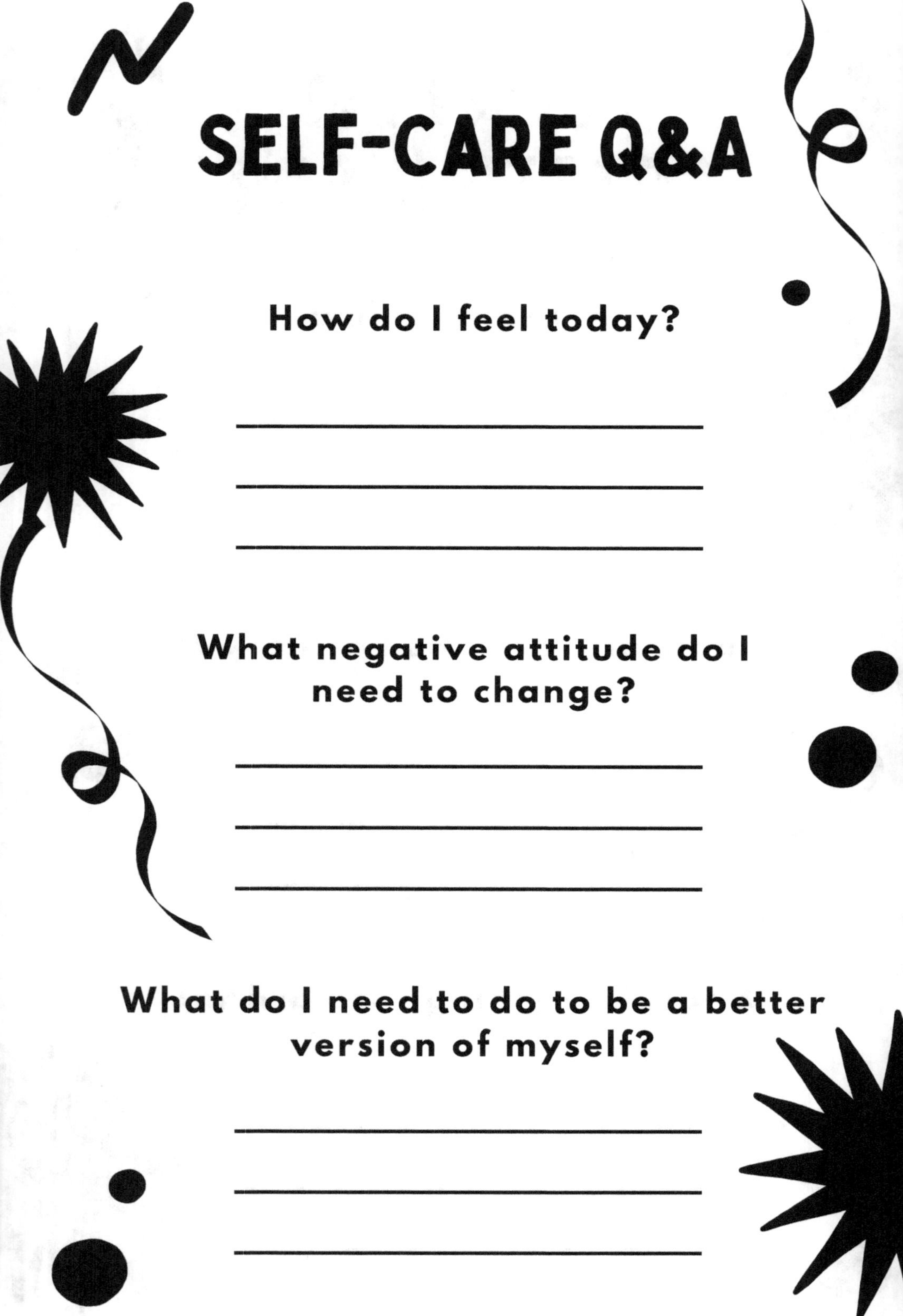

SELF-CARE Q&A

How do I feel today?

____

____

____

What negative attitude do I need to change?

____

____

____

What do I need to do to be a better version of myself?

____

____

____

TODAY I'M GRATEFUL FOR

I'm thankful for:

____

____

____

Goals and dreams I achieved:

____

____

____

What I'm looking forward to:

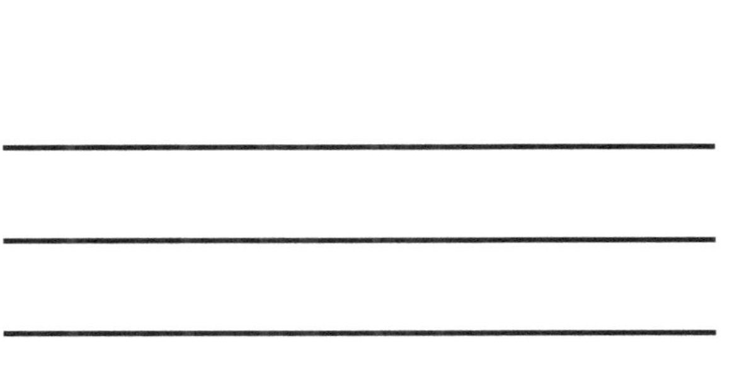

____

____

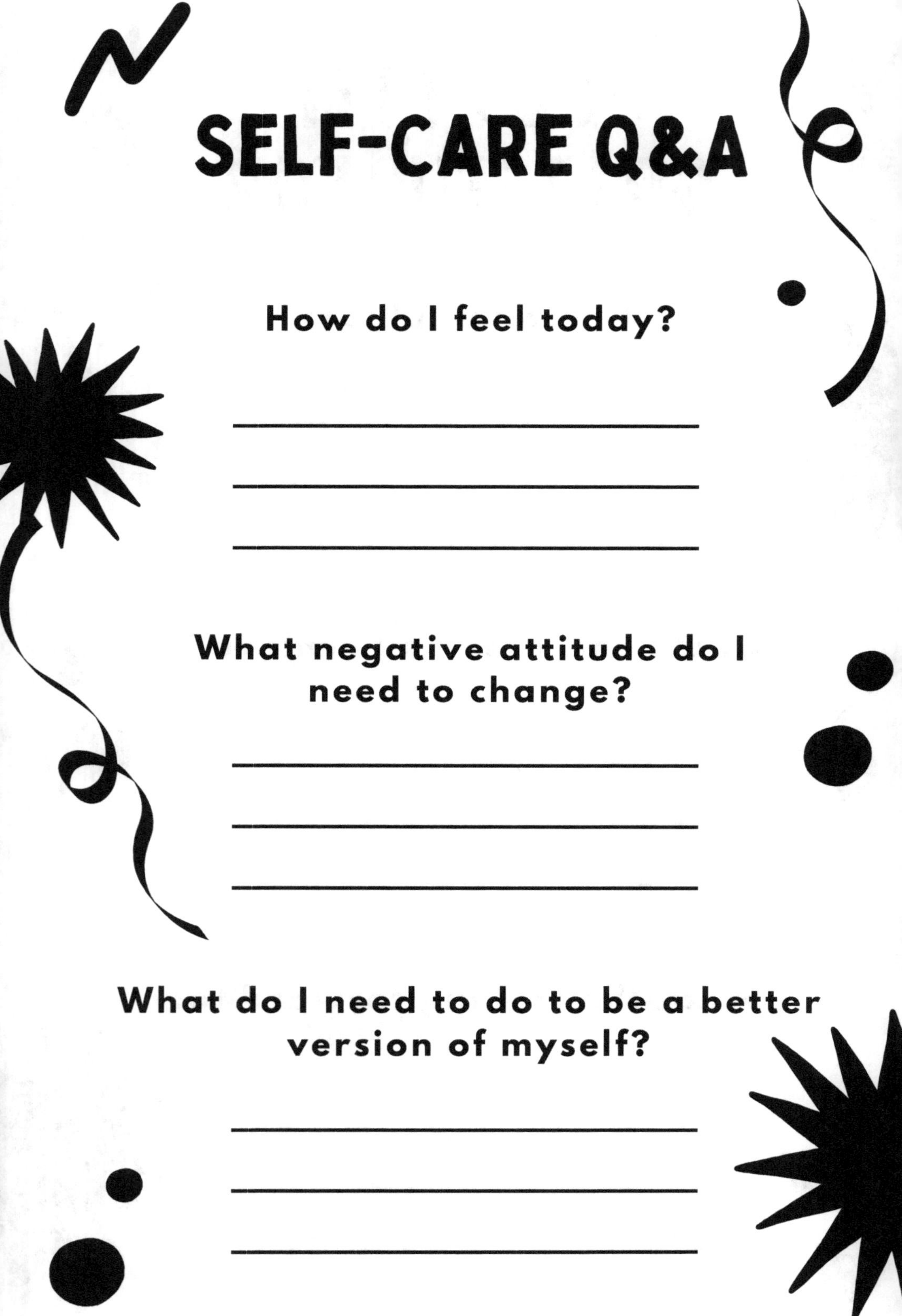

SELF-CARE Q&A

How do I feel today?

What negative attitude do I
need to change?

What do I need to do to be a better
version of myself?

TODAY I'M GRATEFUL FOR

I'm thankful for:

____

____

____

Goals and dreams I achieved:

____

____

____

What I'm looking forward to:

____

____

____

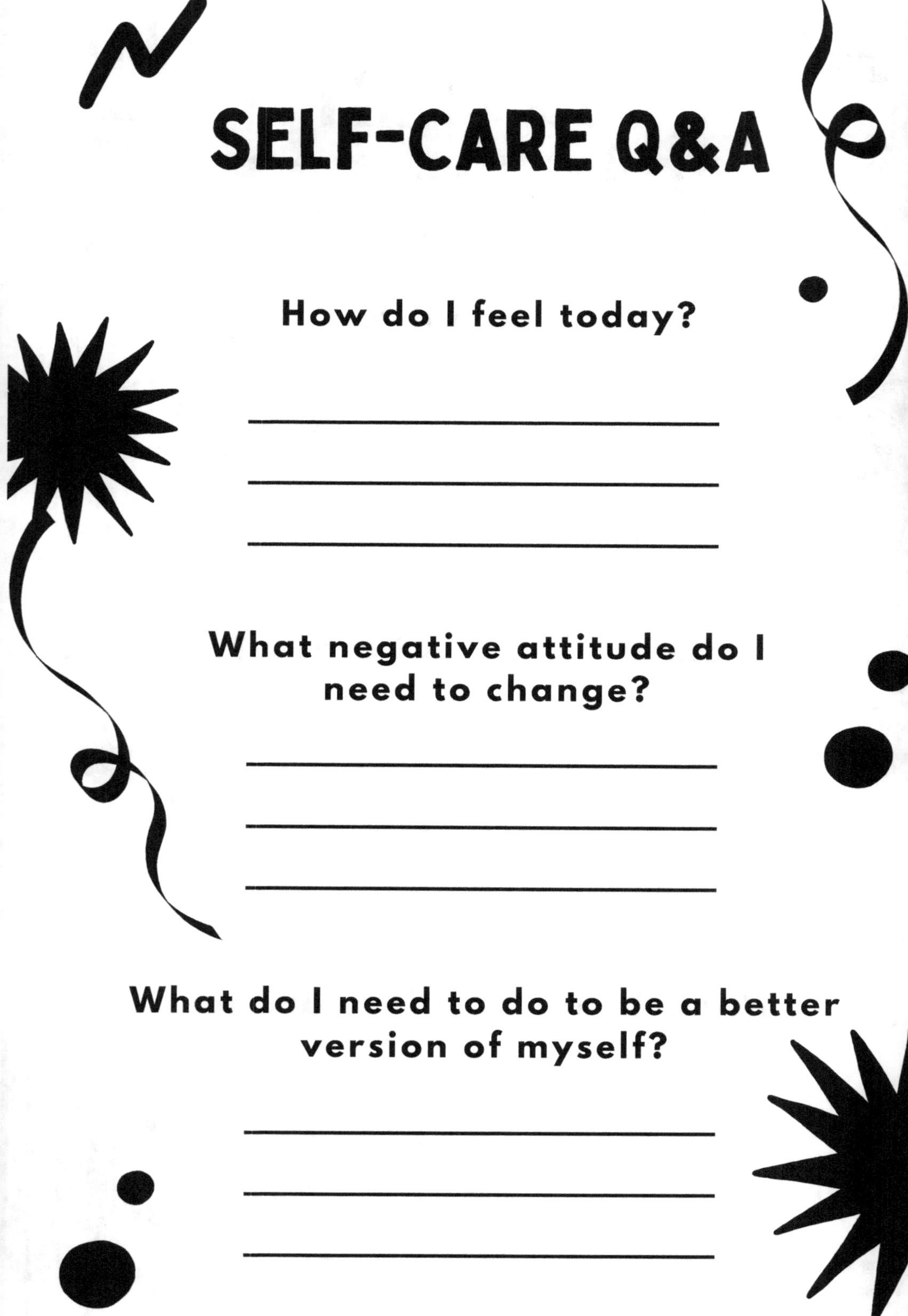

SELF-CARE Q&A

How do I feel today?

What negative attitude do I need to change?

What do I need to do to be a better version of myself?

TODAY I'M GRATEFUL FOR

I'm thankful for:

____

____

____

Goals and dreams I achieved:

____

____

____

What I'm looking forward to:

____

____

____

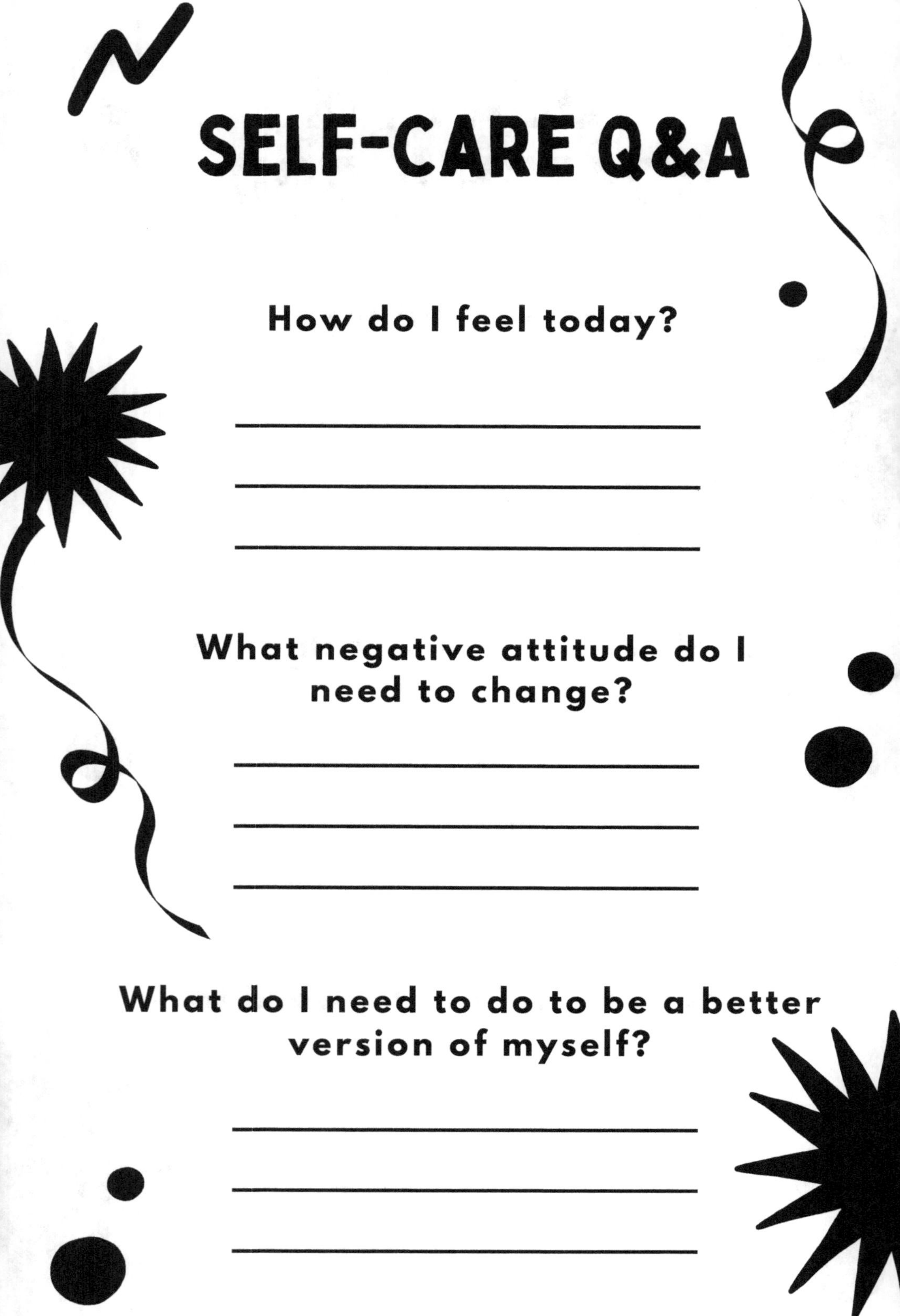

SELF-CARE Q&A

How do I feel today?

____

____

____

What negative attitude do I need to change?

____

____

____

What do I need to do to be a better version of myself?

____

____

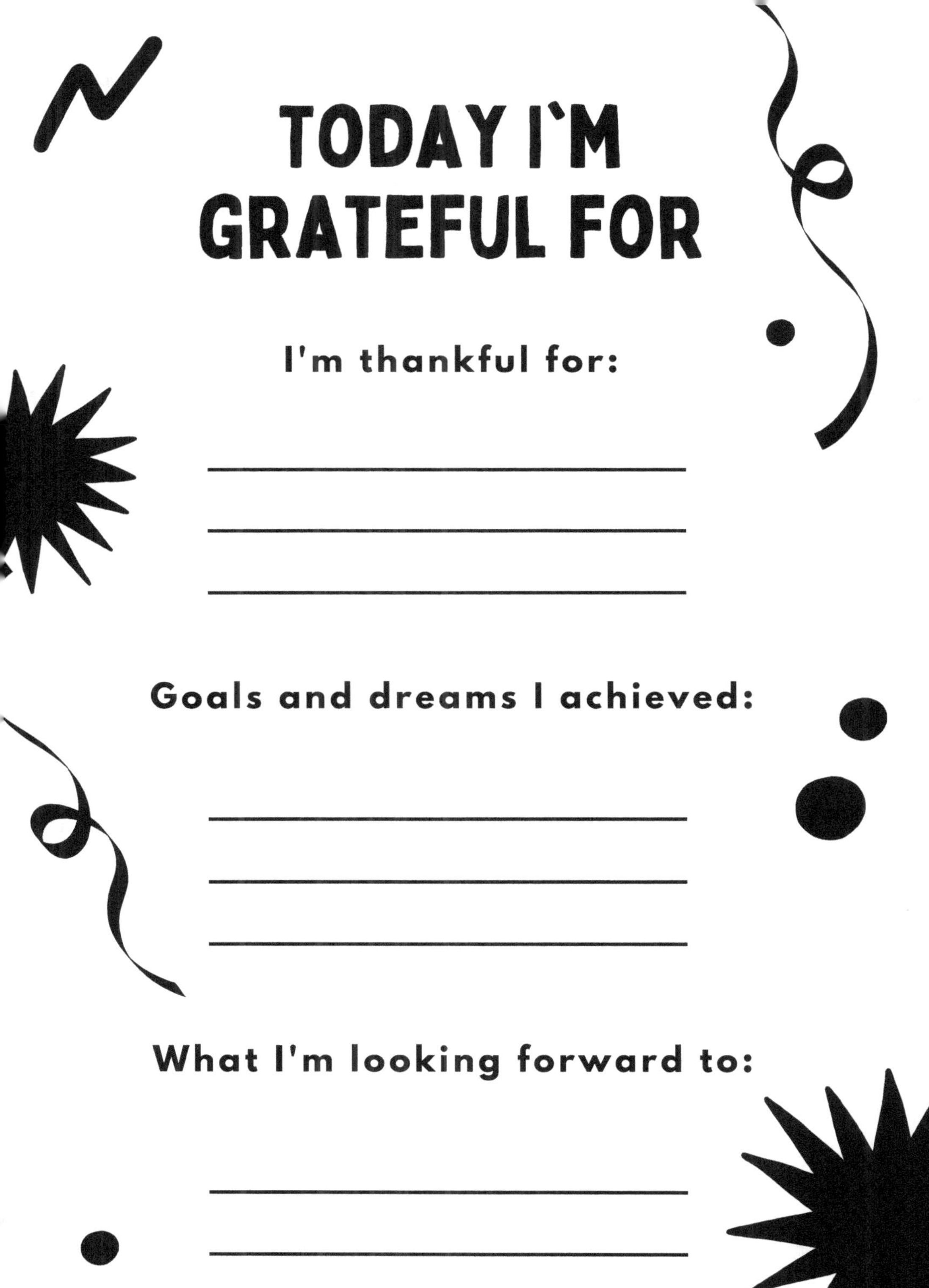

TODAY I'M GRATEFUL FOR

I'm thankful for:

Goals and dreams I achieved:

What I'm looking forward to:

SELF-CARE Q&A

How do I feel today?

What negative attitude do I need to change?

What do I need to do to be a better version of myself?

TODAY I'M GRATEFUL FOR

I'm thankful for:

____

____

____

Goals and dreams I achieved:

____

____

____

What I'm looking forward to:

____

____

____

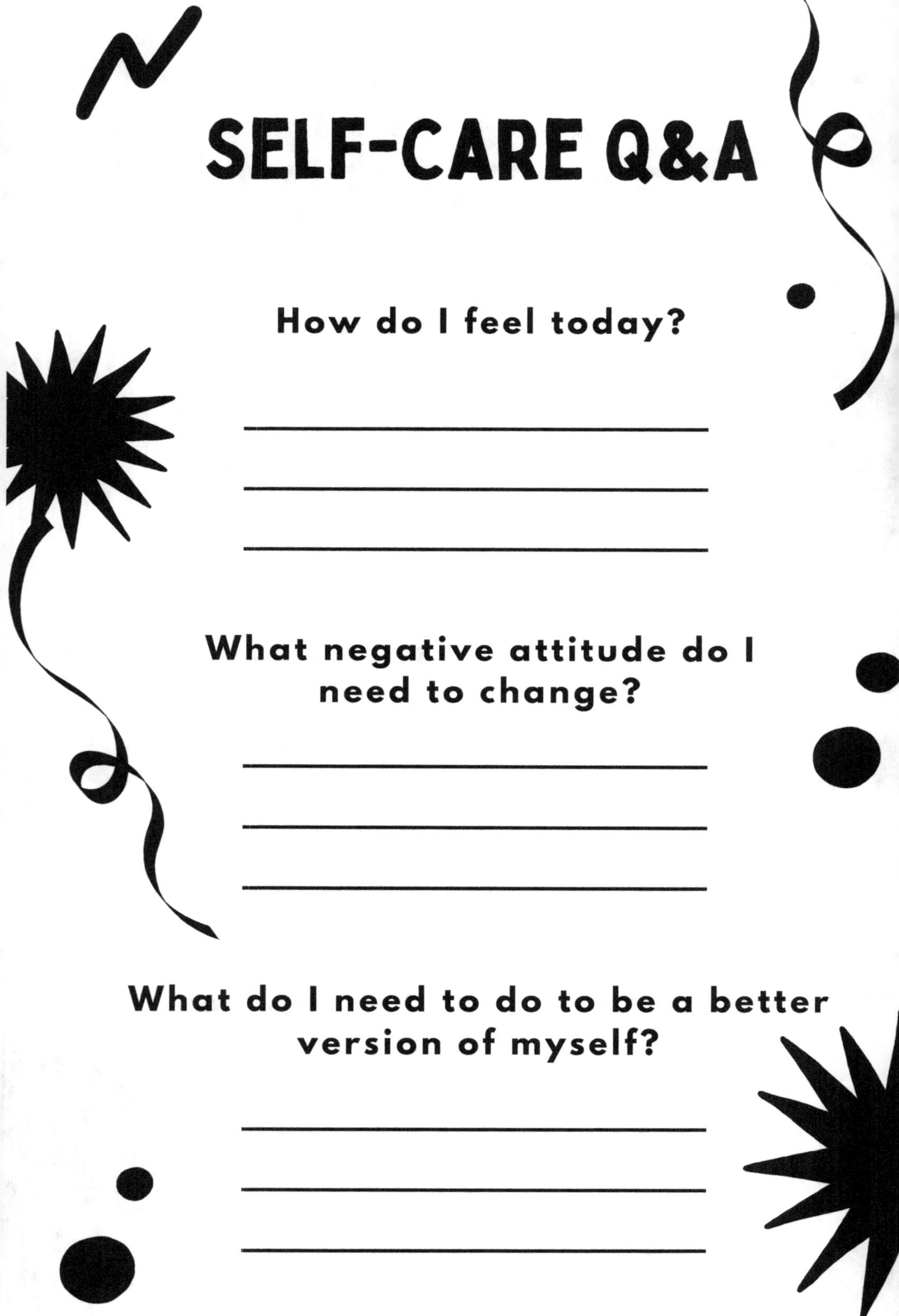

SELF-CARE Q&A

How do I feel today?

What negative attitude do I
need to change?

What do I need to do to be a better
version of myself?

TODAY I'M GRATEFUL FOR

I'm thankful for:

Goals and dreams I achieved:

What I'm looking forward to:

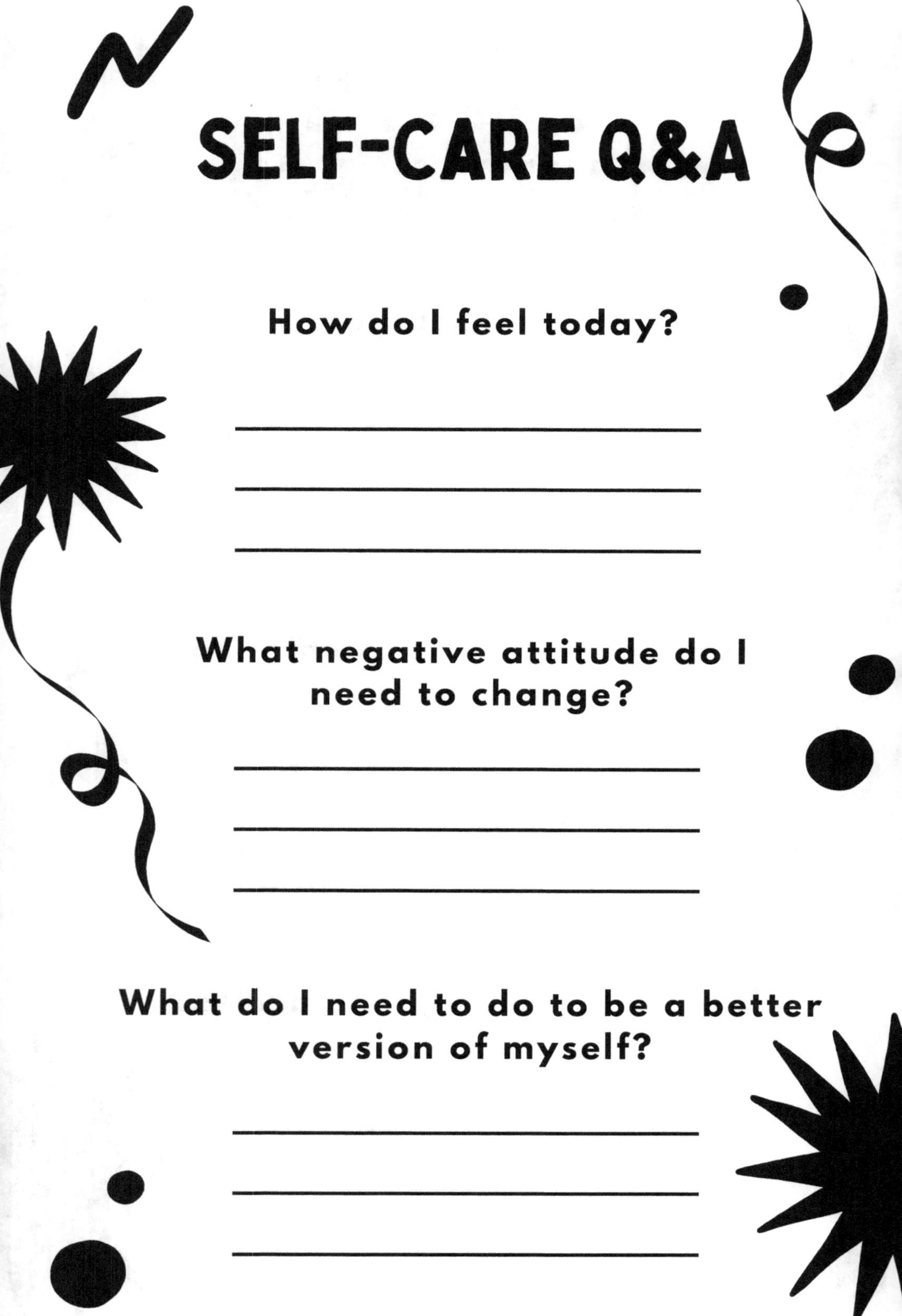

SELF-CARE Q&A
How do I feel today?
What negative attitude do I need to change?
What do I need to do to be a better version of myself?

TODAY I'M GRATEFUL FOR

I'm thankful for:

____

____

____

Goals and dreams I achieved:

____

____

____

What I'm looking forward to:

____

____

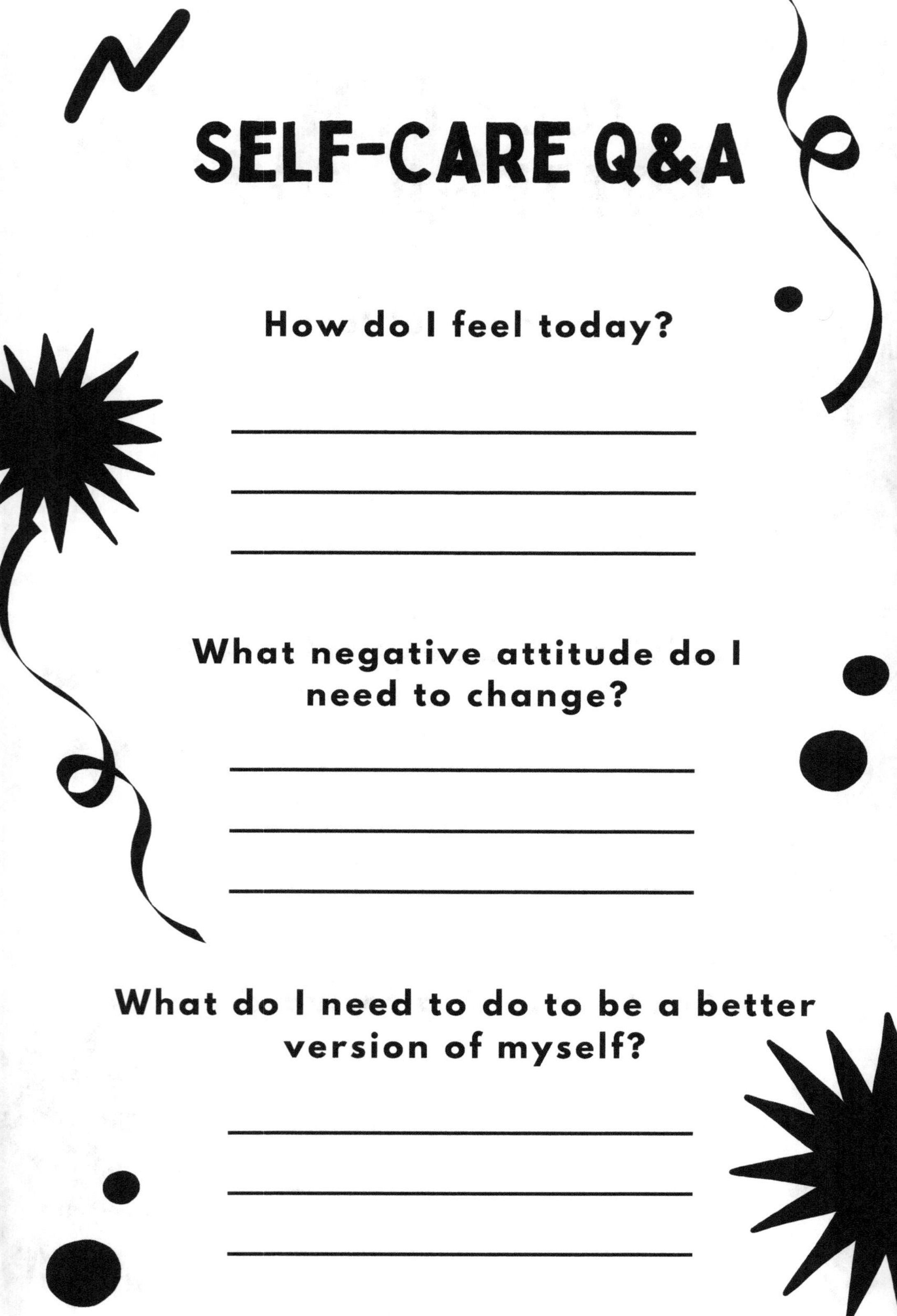

SELF-CARE Q&A

How do I feel today?

____

____

____

What negative attitude do I need to change?

____

____

____

What do I need to do to be a better version of myself?

____

____

____

TODAY I'M GRATEFUL FOR

I'm thankful for:

____

____

____

Goals and dreams I achieved:

____

____

____

What I'm looking forward to:

____

____

____

SELF-CARE Q&A
How do I feel today?
What negative attitude do I need to change?
What do I need to do to be a better version of myself?

TODAY I'M GRATEFUL FOR

I'm thankful for:

____

____

____

Goals and dreams I achieved:

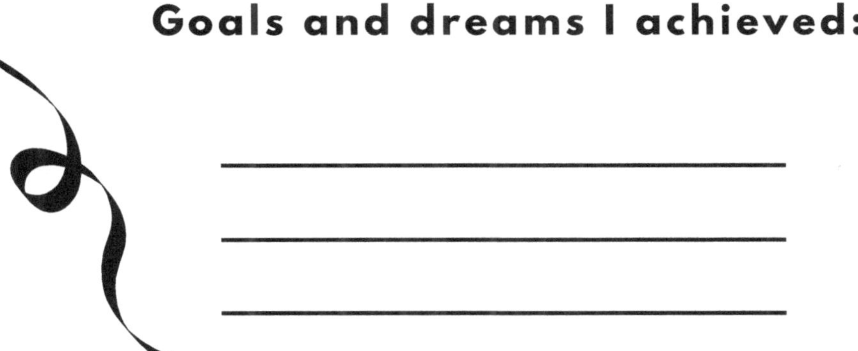

____

____

____

What I'm looking forward to:

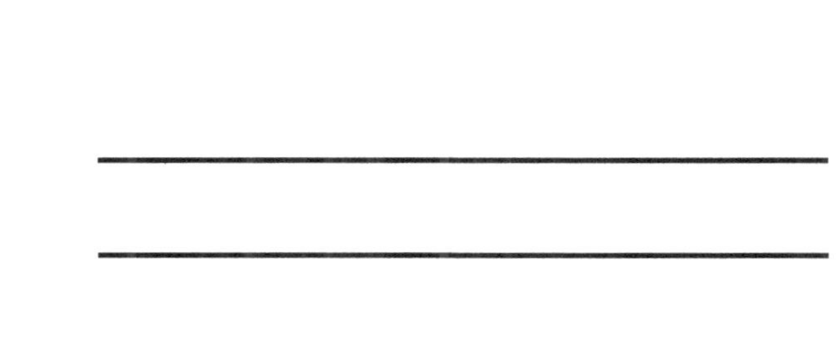

____

____

____

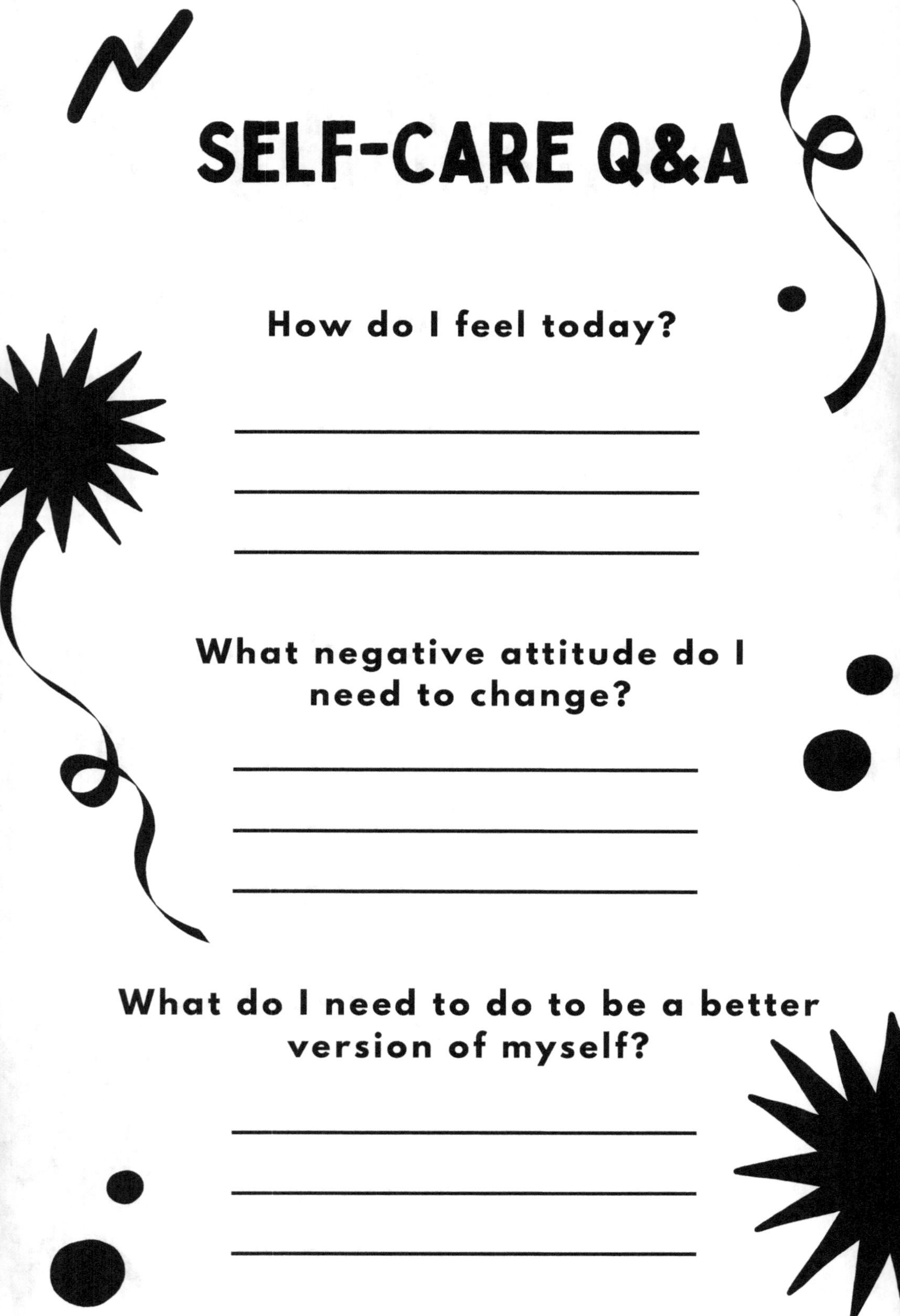

SELF-CARE Q&A

How do I feel today?

What negative attitude do I need to change?

What do I need to do to be a better version of myself?

TODAY I'M GRATEFUL FOR

I'm thankful for:

____

____

____

Goals and dreams I achieved:

____

____

____

What I'm looking forward to:

____

____

____

SELF-CARE Q&A

How do I feel today?

____

____

____

**What negative attitude do I
need to change?**

____

____

____

**What do I need to do to be a better
version of myself?**

____

____

____

TODAY I'M GRATEFUL FOR

I'm thankful for:

____

____

____

Goals and dreams I achieved:

____

____

____

What I'm looking forward to:

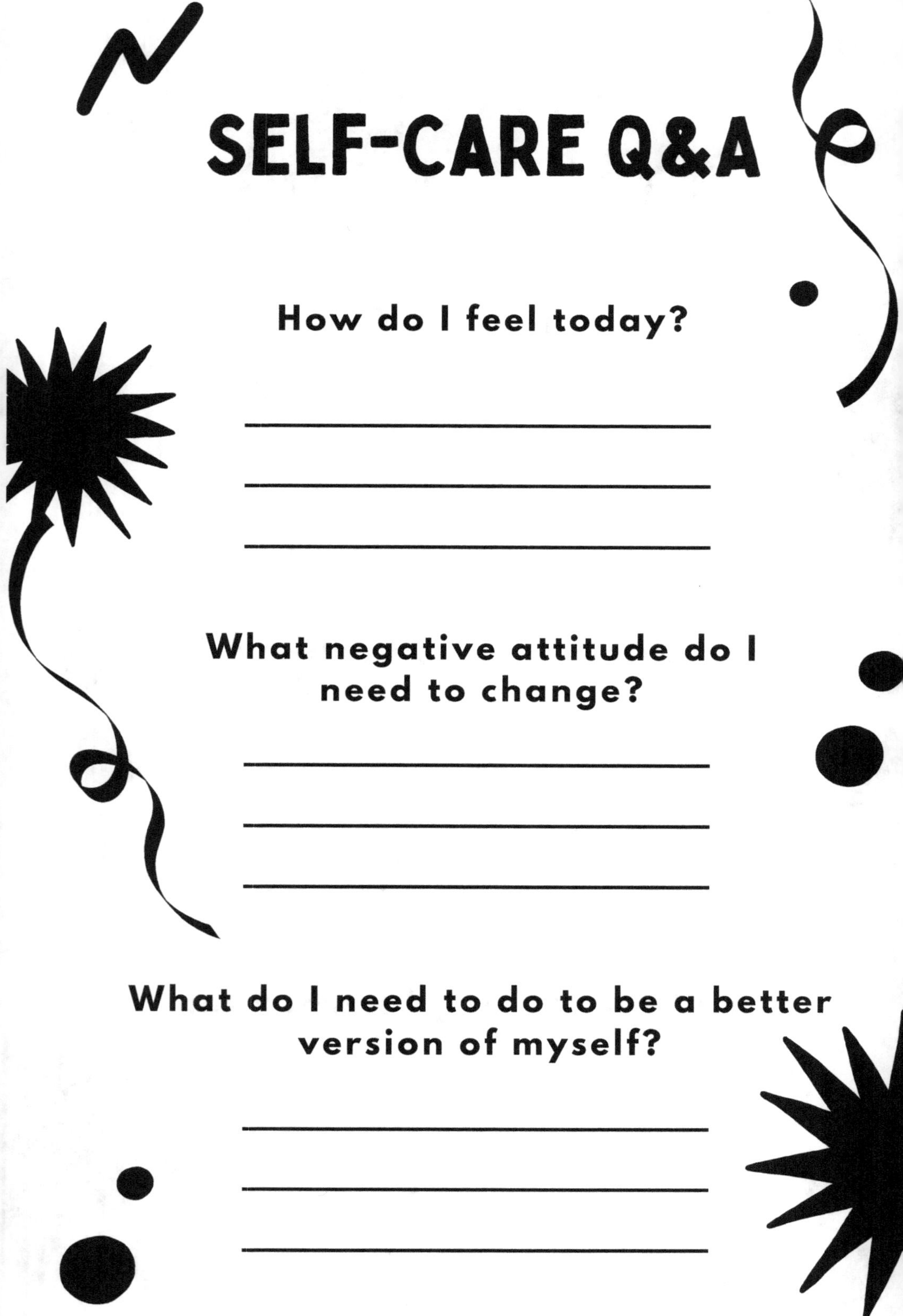

SELF-CARE Q&A

How do I feel today?

____

____

____

What negative attitude do I need to change?

____

____

____

What do I need to do to be a better version of myself?

____

____

____

Thank you.

We hope you enjoyed our journal.

As a small family company, your feedback is very important to us.

Please let us know how you like our journal at:

mollymcluke@gmail.com